Honk, Honk, Rattle, Rattle

Pam Schiller

Special Needs Adaptations by Clarissa Willis

Acknowledgments

I would like to thank the following people for their contributions to this book. The special needs adaptations were written by Clarissa Willis. The CD is arranged by Patrick

Clarissa Willis   Patrick Brennan   Richele Bartkowiak

Brennan, and performed by Richele Bartkowiak and Patrick Brennan. It was engineered and mixed by Jeff Smith at Southwest Recordings. —Pam Schiller

Books written by Pam Schiller

The Bilingual Book of Rhymes, Songs, Stories, and Fingerplays, with Rafael Lara-Alecio and Beverly J. Irby

The Complete Book of Activities, Games, Stories, Props, Recipes, and Dances, with Jackie Silberg

The Complete Book of Rhymes, Songs, Poems, Fingerplays, and Chants, with Jackie Silberg

The Complete Daily Curriculum for Early Childhood: Over 1200 Easy Activities to Support Multiple Intelligences and Learning Styles, with Pat Phipps

The Complete Resource Book: An Early Childhood Curriculum, with Kay Hastings

The Complete Resource Book for Infants: Over 700 Experiences for Children From Birth to 18 Months

The Complete Resource Book for Toddlers and Twos: Over 2000 Experiences and Ideas

Count on Math: Activities for Small Hands and Lively Minds, with Lynne Peterson

Creating Readers: Over 1000 Games, Activities, Tongue Twisters, Fingerplays, Songs, and Stories to Get Children Excited About Reading

Do You Know the Muffin Man?, with Thomas Moore

The Instant Curriculum, Revised, with Joan Rosanno

The Practical Guide to Quality Child Care, with Patricia Carter Dyke

Start Smart: Building Brain Power in the Early Years

The Values Book, with Tamera Bryant

Where Is Thumbkin?, with Thomas Moore

Honk, Honk, Rattle, Rattle

CD INSIDE!

25 Songs and Over 300 Activities for Young Children

Pam Schiller

Gryphon House, Inc.
Beltsville, Maryland

Honk, Honk, Rattle, Rattle

© 2006 Pam Schiller
Printed in the United States of America.

Illustrations: Deborah Johnson
Cover Photograph: Getty Images, ©2005.

Published by Gryphon House, Inc.
10726 Tucker Street, Beltsville, MD 20705
301.595.9500; 301.595.0051 (fax); 800.638.0928 (toll-free)

Visit us on the web at www.ghbooks.com

 Gryphon House is a member of the Green Press Initiative, a nonprofit program dedicated to supporting publishers in their efforts to reduce their use of fiber sourced forests. For further information visit www.greenpressinitiative.org

Library of Congress Cataloging-in-Publication Data

Schiller, Pamela Byrne.
  Honk, honk, rattle, rattle / Pam Schiller and Richele Bartkowiak ; special needs adaptations by Clarissa Willis.
      p. cm.
  Includes bibliographical references.
  ISBN-13: 978-0-87659-018-8
  ISBN-10: 0-87659-018-0
 1. Music--Instruction and study--Juvenile. 2. School music--Instruction and study--Activity programs. 3. Early childhood education. 4. Children's songs. 5. Education, Preschool. I. Bartkowiak, Richele. II. Willis, Clarissa. III. Title.
  MT920.S39 2006
  372.87'044--dc22

                                    2006007256

Table of Contents

Before serving food to children, be aware of children's food allergies and sensitivities, as well as any religious or cultural practices that exclude certain foods. Be sure to incorporate this information into your daily planning.

Introduction

Music in the Early Years

Music is a universal language, and singing is a hallmark of the early childhood classroom. Children love to sing! Teachers love to sing! Age makes no difference. Culture makes no difference.

Singing songs enriches thematic content, supports literacy concepts, and optimizes memory and learning. When you extend classroom activities, including modifications for special needs and English language learner populations, it is a perfect package. *Honk, Honk, Rattle, Rattle* is one of eight thematic book/CD sets that offer all of these resources in one package.

Thematic Content

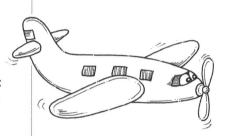

Honk, Honk, Rattle, Rattle draws on several typical early childhood themes: Transportation, Travel, Parts of the Body, and Sounds. Read the lyrics of the songs and decide which songs best fit in your curriculum

Every song is accompanied by a list of facts titled "Did You Know?" which offers background information about the song, interesting facts about the topic or lyrics, historical information, or some form of trivia you can use as a springboard to discussion. This will save you hours of research and add significantly to the value of the song.

Literacy Concepts

Young children need experiences that allow them to develop and practice basic literacy skills, such as listening, oral language development, phonological awareness, letter knowledge, print awareness, and comprehension. Suggestions for using the songs in *Honk, Honk, Rattle, Rattle* as a springboard for teaching these literacy skills accompany every title. Below is a definition of each literacy skill and the sub-skills they encompass.

- ○ **Listening:** the development of age-appropriate attention span, as well as the ability to listen for a variety of purposes; for example, details, directions, and sounds.

- ○ **Oral Language Development:** the acquisition of vocabulary, the fine-tuning of grammar, and the increase in sentence length and complexity.

○ **Phonological Awareness:** sensitivity to the sounds of language. Phonological awareness begins with babbling and cooing and goes all the way through the understanding of sound and symbol relationships and decoding. The skills in the higher end of the phonological awareness continuum—sound and symbol relationship and decoding—are appropriate for children who are age five or older.

○ **Segmentation:** the breaking apart of words by syllable or letter; for example, children clap the breaks in the word *di-no-saur.*

○ **Rhyme:** words that sound alike. The ending sound of the words is the same, but the initial consonant sound is different, for example, *cat* and *hat,* or *rake* and *cake.*

○ **Alliteration:** the repetition of a consonant sound in a series of words; for example, Peter Piper picked a peck of pickled peppers. Children need to be able to hear the repetition of the /p/ sound, but do not need to identify that the sound is made by the letter "p".

○ **Onomatopoeia:** words that imitate the sound they are describing; for example, *pitter-patter, moo, quack, beep,* and so on.

○ **Letter Knowledge:** the visual recognition of each letter of the alphabet, both lowercase and uppercase.

○ **Print Awareness:** the understanding that print has many functions; for example, telling a story, making a list, as part of signs, in news articles, in recipes, and so on. It is also the awareness that print moves left to right and top to bottom.

○ **Comprehension:** the internalization of a story or a concept.

Optimizing Memory and Learning

Singing boosts memory and keeps the brain alert. Increased memory and alertness optimize the potential for learning. When we sing we generally feel good. That sense of well-being causes the brain to release endorphins into the blood stream and those endorphins act as a memory fixative. When we sing we automatically increase our oxygen intake, which, in turn, increases our alertness. Scientific research has validated what early childhood professionals know intuitively—that singing has a positive effect on learning.

Expanding Children's Learning With Activities

Using songs as a springboard for activities is a good way to bring the lyrics of the song into a meaningful context for children. Exploring canoes in the sand and water center after singing "Little Canoe" reinforces and creates meaningful context for the specific characteristics of this type of boat. Making "box sleighs," creating snow pictures, moving items across a tray of ice, and stringing bells after singing "Jingle Bells" helps children better understand the characteristics of ice and snow, as well as the characteristics of travel over ice.

Reading a book about sleigh travel after singing about sleigh travel also helps expand children's understanding. Exploring different types of clothing after singing a song about winter clothes reinforces and creates a meaningful context for the specific characteristics of winter clothing. Literature selections are provided for each song. Integrating the teaching of themes and skills with songs, literature, and multidisciplinary activities provides a comprehensive approach for helping children recognize the patterns and the interconnected relationships of what they are learning.

Throughout the book, questions to ask children appear in italics. These questions are intended to help children think and reflect on what they have learned. This reflective process optimizes the opportunity for children to apply the information and experiences they have encountered.

Modifications

Suggestions for children with special needs and suggestions for English language learners accompany the song activities when appropriate. These features allow teachers to use the activities with diverse populations. All children love to sing and the benefits apply to all!

Special Needs

The inclusion of children with disabilities in preschool and child care programs is increasingly common. Parents, teachers, and researchers have found that children benefit in many ways from integrated programs that are designed to meet the needs of all children. Many children with disabilities, however, need accommodations to participate successfully in the general classroom.

Included in the extensions and activities for each song are adaptations for children with special needs. These adaptations allow *all* children to experience the song and related activities in a way that will maximize their learning opportunities. The adaptations are specifically for children who have needs in the following areas:

❍ sensory integration
❍ distractibility
❍ hearing loss
❍ spatial organization
❍ language, receptive and expressive
❍ fine motor coordination
❍ cognitive challenges

The following general strategies from Kathleen Bulloch (2003) are for children who have difficulty listening and speaking.

Difficulty	Adaptations/Modifications/Strategies
Listening	○ State the objective—provide a reason for listening. ○ Use a photo card. ○ Give explanations in small, discrete steps. ○ Be concise with verbal information: "Evan, please sit," instead of "Evan, would you please sit down in your chair?" ○ Provide visuals. ○ Have the child repeat directions. ○ Have the child close his eyes and try to visualize the information. ○ Provide manipulative tasks. ○ When giving directions to the class, leave a pause between each step so the child can carry out the process in her mind. ○ Shorten the listening time required. ○ Pre-teach difficult vocabulary and concepts.
Verbal Expression	○ Provide a prompt, such as beginning the sentence for the child or giving a picture cue. ○ Accept an alternate form of information-sharing, such as artistic creation, photos, charade or pantomime, and demonstration. ○ Ask questions that require short answers. ○ Specifically teach body and language expression. ○ First ask questions at the information level—giving facts and asking for facts back. ○ Wait for children to respond; don't call on the first child to raise his hand. ○ Have the child break in gradually by speaking in smaller groups and then in larger groups.

English Language Learners

Strategies for English language learners are also provided to maximize their learning potential.

The following are general strategies for working with English language learners (Gray, Fleischman, 2004-05):

○ **Keep the language simple.** Speak simply and clearly. Use short, complete sentences in a normal tone of voice. Avoid using slang, idioms, or figures of speech.

○ **Use actions and illustrations to reinforce oral statements.** Appropriate prompts and facial expressions help convey meaning.

○ **Ask for completion, not generation.** Ask children to choose answers from a list or to complete a partially finished sentence. Encourage children to use language as much as possible to gain confidence over time.

○ **Model correct usage and judiciously correct errors.** Use corrections to positively reinforce children's use of English. When English language learners make a mistake or use awkward language, they are often attempting to apply what they know about their first language to English. For example, a Spanish-speaking child may say, "It fell from me," a direct translation from Spanish, instead of "I dropped it."

○ **Use visual aids.** Present classroom content and information in a way that engages children—by using graphic organizers (word web, story maps, KWL charts), photographs, concrete materials, and graphs, for example.

Involving English Language Learners in Music Activities

Music is a universal language that draws people together. For English language learners, music can be a powerful vehicle for language learning and community-building. Music and singing are important to second language learners for many reasons, including:

○ The rhythms of music help children hear the sounds and intonation patterns of a new language.

○ Musical lyrics and accompanying motions help children learn new vocabulary.

○ Repetitive patterns of language in songs help children internalize the sentence structure of English.

○ Important cultural information is conveyed to young children in the themes of songs.

Strategies for involving English language learners in music activities vary according to the children's level of proficiency in the English language.

Level of Proficiency	Strategies
Beginning English Language Learners	o Keep the child near you and model motions as you engage in group singing. o Use hand gestures, movements, and signs as often as possible to accompany song lyrics, making sure to tie a specific motion to a specific word. o Refer to real objects in the environment that are named in a song. o Stress the intonation, sounds, and patterns in language by speaking the lyrics of the song while performing actions or referring to objects in the environment. o Use simple, more common vocabulary. For example, use *round* instead of *circular.*
Intermediate-Level English Language Learners	o Say the song before singing it, so children can hear the words and rhythms of the lyrics. o Use motions, gestures, and signs to help children internalize the meaning of song lyrics. Be sure the motion is tied clearly to the associated word. o Throughout the day, repeat the language patterns found in songs in various activities. o Stress the language patterns in songs, and pause as children fill in the blanks. o Adapt the patterns of the song, using familiar vocabulary.
Advanced English Language Learners	o Use visuals to cue parts of a song. o Use graphic organizers to introduce unfamiliar information. o Use synonyms for words heard in songs to expand children's vocabulary. o Develop vocabulary through description and comparison. For example, it is *round* like a circle. It is *circular.* o Encourage children to make up new lyrics for songs.

How to Use This Book

Use the 25 songs on the *Honk, Honk, Rattle, Rattle* CD that is included with this book, and the related activities in the book, to enhance themes in your curriculum, or use them independently. Either way you have a rich treasure chest of creative ideas for your classroom.

The eight package collection provides more than 200 songs, a perfect combination of the traditional best-loved children's songs and brand new selections created for each theme. Keep a song in your heart and put joy in your teaching!

Bibliography

Bulloch, K. 2003. *The mystery of modifying: Creative solutions.* Huntsville, TX: Education Service Center, Region VI.

Cavallaro, C. & M. Haney. 1999. *Preschool inclusion.* Baltimore, MD: Paul H. Brookes Publishing Company.

Gray, T. and S. Fleischman. Dec. 2004-Jan. 2005. "Research matters: Successful strategies for English language learners." *Educational Leadership,* 62, 84-85.

Hanniford, C. 1995. *Smart moves: Why learning is not all in your head.* Arlington, VA: Great Ocean Publications, p. 146.

LeDoux, J. 1993. "Emotional memory systems in the brain." *Behavioral and Brain Research,* 58.

Tabors, P. 1997. *One child, two languages: Children learning English as a second language.* Baltimore, MD: Paul H. Brookes Publishing Company.

HONK, HONK, RATTLE, RATTLE

Songs and Activities

Honk, Honk, Rattle, Rattle

additional verses by Pam Schiller

(Tune: I'm a Little Acorn Brown)
I'm a little hunk of tin.
Nobody knows what shape
    I'm in.
Got four wheels and a tank
    of gas.
I can go but not too fast.

Chorus:
Honk, honk
Rattle, rattle, rattle.
Crash, beep, beep.
Honk, honk
Rattle, rattle, rattle.
Crash, beep, beep.

I'm a little ice cream truck
I wibble, wobble like a duck.
Got four wheels and lots
    of cream,
I make children shout and
    scream.

(Chorus)

I'm a little yellow bus,
Newly painted, not a spot
    of rust,
Brand new wheels and
    kids inside
Hold on tight for a happy ride.

(Chorus)

Vocabulary

beep
bus
crash
cream
gas
honk
hunk of tin
ice cream
rust
shape
rattle
tank
truck
wheel
wibble
wobble

Theme Connections

Movement
Sound

Did You Know?

○ Contrary to popular belief, Henry Ford did not invent the automobile. What Ford did was perfect the assembly line technique. This allowed him to lower the cost of the automobile drastically, bringing a rich man's plaything within reach of the masses, thereby changing Western society. The original lyrics of "Little Hunk of Tin" refer to a Ford ("I'm a 4-door, I'm a Ford").

○ In 1860 a Frenchman, Edouard Delamare-Debouteville, did some experiments and filed patents for a self-propelled car. In 1884, France built the world's first car. However, the first self-propelled vehicle existed long before 1884.

○ Steam-powered stage coaches were in regular service between many towns in Britain from 1820 to 1840.

○ There are over 200 million cars on US highways today.

○ The sedan remains the most popular car type, with hatchbacks and SUVs placed second and third.

Literacy Links

Oral Language
○ Discuss the likenesses and differences between buses and cars.
○ Discuss types of cars: sedans, hatchbacks, SUVs, and trucks.
○ Point out the synonyms for *hunk of tin* (car, automobile, and vehicle).
○ Teach the children the American Sign Language sign for *car* (page 120).

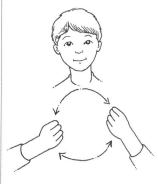

car

Oral Language/Phonological Awareness
○ Sing "The Wheels on the Bus" changing *bus* to *car*. *Does changing the type of vehicle change the verses?*

Phonological Awareness
○ Discuss the *onomatopoeic* words (words that sound like their meaning) in the song, such as *honk, rattle, crash,* and *beep.*

Print Awareness
○ Discuss the print found on cars. *Where is the make and model located? What does the print on the radio tell us? What are the letters and numbers on the license plate for?*

Curriculum Connections

Blocks
○ Provide several small cars for the center. Encourage the children to build highways, garages, and/or parking lots.

Special Needs Adaptation: Block play provides an excellent opportunity to learn collaboration while developing both motor and problem-solving skills. Children with motor skill issues, especially those with cerebral palsy, may be unable to roll a toy car back and forth. To help the child manipulate the cars more easily, attach a small wooden knob (found in hardware stores) or a plastic drawer handle to the top of the car. The handle or knob can be attached easily with hot glue. Children can use the knob or handle to move their car down the road or through the tunnels they build with the blocks.

Book Corner

Duck in the Truck by
    Jez Alborough
*Mike Mulligan and
    His Steam Shovel*
    by Virginia Lee
    Burton
Sheep in a Jeep by
    Nancy Shaw

Discovery

○ Use masking tape to secure a marker to the back of a small car. Provide butcher paper and encourage the children to drive the vehicle across the paper to create car tracks. *What happens when you turn? What happens when you go backwards?*

Gross Motor

○ Crumple aluminum foil into balls. Create a throw line by placing a strip of masking tape on the floor. Provide a metal bucket, if possible, or a basket or box and encourage the children to toss the "tin balls" into the bucket or box. Discuss the characteristics of aluminium foil, which are similar to tin. *Is it heavy or light? What sound does it make when it lands in the bucket? What sound does it make when it lands on the floor?*

Listening

○ Provide several potato chip cans along with a handful of buttons, washers, pennies, toothpicks, and beads. Encourage the children to fill the cans to create different rattle sounds. *Which item is the heaviest? Which make the loudest sound? Which makes the softest sound?*

Math

○ Provide a honking toy, beeping toy, cymbals, and a rattle. Encourage the children to create a pattern of honks, beeps, crashes, and rattles.
○ Create a graph showing various car colors. Invite the children to note the color of one of their family cars on the graph by marking the correct column with a Post-it note. *Which is the most popular color of vehicle?*

Writing

○ Provide old license plates, crayons, and paper. Encourage the children to rub the plates to create license plate rubbings. Challenge the children to use blank paper to create their own license plates.

Home Connection

○ Encourage the children to talk with their families about the family car. *What kind of car is it? What make and model? What color is the car? Where did the car come from?* Be sure to allow children to report the information they gathered.

If I Had Wings

Vocabulary

breeze
butterfly
clouds
floating
fly
hills
mountain
rolling
watching
wings

Theme Connections

Me
Things I Like
Travel

If I had the wings of an airplane
Up to the hills I would fly.
Flying around in the sweet
    breeze,
Watching the clouds rolling by.
Oooh lah lah, oooh lah lah,
    oooh lah lay,
Oooh lah lah, oooh lah lah lay.
Oooh lah lah, oooh lah lah,
    oooh lah lay,
Oooh lah lah, oooh lah lah lay.

If I had the wings of a butterfly
Up to the mountains I'd fly.
Floating around on the sweet
    breeze,
Watching the clouds rolling by.
Oooh lah lah, oooh lah lah,
    oooh lah lay,
Oooh lah lah, oooh lah lah lay.
Oooh lah lah, oooh lah lah,
    oooh lah lay,
Oooh lah lah, oooh lah lah lay.
Oooh lah lah, oooh lah lah lay.

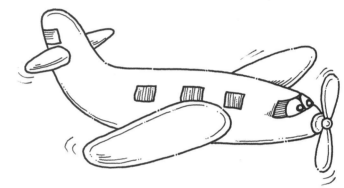

Did You Know?

○ Lift is the aerodynamic force that counteracts gravity and holds an airplane
  in the air. Most of the lift required by an airplane is created by its wings,
  but a certain portion is also generated by other parts of the aircraft, such as
  the fuselage.

○ Butterfly and moth wings are marvelously elaborate structures of
  membranes no more than two cells thick. The shape and size of wings
  varies between species and takes on a characteristic shape that may
  include scalloping, lobes, and even hair-like slivers.

Literacy Links

Comprehension

○ Teach the children songs, fingerplays, and action rhymes about airplanes
  (pages 94-96).

airplane

Oral Language
○ Discuss other things that fly (for example, bumblebees, birds, butterflies, helicopters, and bees). Sing a new verse of the song substituting "bumblebee" or any other thing that flies for "airplane."
○ Discuss unusual phrases in the songs such as "sweet breeze" and "clouds rolling by."
○ Teach the children the American Sign Language signs for *airplane* and *butterfly* (page 120).

Phonological Awareness
○ Substitute the syllable "moo" for "oooh" and "ma" for "lah." Sing the song again with new sounds. Try other syllable substitutions.

Print Awareness
○ Print "oooh lah lah" on chart paper. Encourage the children to identify the letters. *Which letter is part of both words? Which word has three of the same letter?*

Curriculum Connections

Art/Blocks
○ Encourage the children to build a house with blocks on the floor. Have them stand over the house and draw a picture of the house from this different perspective.

Blocks/Language
○ Help the children build an airport. Encourage them to build the control tower, runway terminals, and so on. Use as much vocabulary as possible.

Fine Motor/Outdoors
○ Provide paper and have the children color it as they wish. Show them how to fold the paper into an airplane. Fly the planes outdoors.

Gross Motor
○ Place a box on the floor and cover it with a sheet or a towel to make it look like a mountain. Invite the children to "fly" over the mountain by jumping or jumping over the covered box.

Math
○ Use a piece of yarn to measure each child's arm width. Cut the yarn and give it to each child. Have the children use blocks to measure the yarn. "My arm is two blocks wide."

Music and Movement

○ Give children paper plates to hold in each hand to make pretend wings. Encourage them to decorate their wings with crayons, markers, and paint. Play classical music and encourage them to use the wings to "fly."

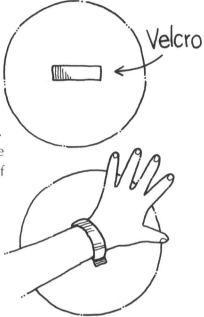

Velcro

Special Needs Adaptation: For children with special needs, use large paper plates. When the child has finished decorating his plate, attach a small piece of Velcro to the back of it. Make a cloth bracelet for the child to wear around his wrist. Then on the inside of his wrist, on the cloth bracelet, attach another piece of Velcro. This will allow the child to participate in the activity without having to hold the paper plate. This is especially effective for a child with motor or tactile sensitivity.

Outdoors

○ Take the children outdoors and have them lie on their backs and watch the clouds rolling by. *Do you see any airplanes in the sky? Do you see anything else flying in the sky?*

Science

○ Provide a variety of pictures of animals or use plastic animals. Encourage the children to sort the pictures into animals with "wings" and "no wings."

Writing

○ Print "oooh lah lah" on a sheet of paper and place it in the center of the table. Provide paper and encourage the children to copy the words.

○ See pages 66-68 in "Airplane Flyers" for additional airplane-related activities.

Home Connection

○ Encourage the children to ask their families where they would fly if they had wings. Let children report their findings when they return to school.

Airport by Byron Barton
Flying by Donald Crews
Oh Lord, I Wish I Was a Buzzard by Polly Greenberg

Bumping Up and Down in My Little Red Wagon

Bumping up and down in my little red wagon,
Bumping up and down in my little red wagon,
Bumping up and down in my little red wagon,
Up and down, we're having fun.

Swayin' side to side in my little red wagon,
Swayin' side to side in my little red wagon,
Swayin' side to side in my little red wagon,
Side to side, we're having fun.

Rockin' back and forth in my little red wagon,
Rockin' back and forth in my little red wagon,
Rockin' back and forth in my little red wagon,
Back and forth, we're having fun.

Hey, ho, in my little red wagon,
Hey, ho, in my little red wagon,
Hey, ho, in my little red wagon,
Riding around and having fun!

Vocabulary

back and forth
bumping
little
red
riding
riding around
rocking
side to side
swaying
up and down
wagon

Theme Connections

Spatial Relationships
Toys

Did You Know?

❍ A wagon is a vehicle with four wheels, traditionally pulled by an animal such as horse, mule, or ox, and used to transport heavy goods. It is also a toy. A toy wagon has the same structure as the larger wagon, a box on wheels, but with an open top and much smaller in size. A child's wagon is traditionally painted red. An average toy wagon seats one child, and can be pulled along using the handle at the front.

❍ Two famous wagon brands are Radio Flyer and Red Rider. The child's version of the little red wagon has been around for more than 85 years.

❍ To celebrate the 80th anniversary of the Radio Flyer (the most popular red wagon), the Radio Flyer company created a monument to the wonder of childhood play, The World's Largest Wagon™.

❍ The World's Largest Wagon™ in Chicago, Illinois is nine times the size of the Original Little Red Wagon™ that millions of Americans grew up with. It is 27 feet long, 13 feet wide, with wheels 8 feet in diameter.

Literacy Links

Comprehension

❍ Share the story "My Little Red Wagon" (pages 96-97) with the children. Discuss things one might haul in a little red wagon.

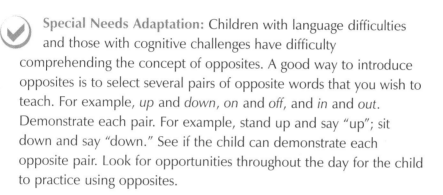

Oral Language

❍ Ask individual children to demonstrate bumping, swaying, and rocking.

❍ Discuss spatial relationship words like *up* and *down*, *back* and *forth*, and so on. Have the children demonstrate the words as you discuss them.

> **Special Needs Adaptation:** Children with language difficulties and those with cognitive challenges have difficulty comprehending the concept of opposites. A good way to introduce opposites is to select several pairs of opposite words that you wish to teach. For example, *up* and *down*, *on* and *off*, and *in* and *out*. Demonstrate each pair. For example, stand up and say "up"; sit down and say "down." See if the child can demonstrate each opposite pair. Look for opportunities throughout the day for the child to practice using opposites.

Phonological Awareness

❍ Encourage the children to think of words that rhyme with *wagon*.

Curriculum Connections

Art

❍ Provide red and black tempera paint and encourage children to paint wagons.

Blocks

❍ Provide blocks and cardboard box lids to use as a wagon. Show the children how to load the "wagons" (box lids) with blocks and then scoot it across the floor.

Discovery

❍ Provide a wagon for children to explore. Encourage them to name the parts of the wagon (for example, handle, wheels, axle, and bed). Suggest that they try spinning the wagon wheels while it is upside down.

❍ Fill a squirt bottle (ketchup style) with sand. Tie an 8' strip of yarn or rope to the bottle and hang it upside down from the ceiling (with the

Book Corner

A Red Wagon Year by
    Kathy Appelt
My Little Wagon by
    Alma Powell
*The Up and Down
    Book* by Mary
    Blair

small cap still on the tip of the bottle). Lay butcher paper or a tablecloth on the floor under the bottle. Remove the lid. Invite the children to swing the bottle and watch the path it takes as the sand falls onto the butcher paper, which is similar to the way a wagon sways from side to side.

Games

❍ Tie a washer to one end of an 18″ piece of yarn. Tie the other end to a coat hanger tube. Place the tube between the seats of two chairs to create a pendulum. Use masking tape to secure the cardboard coat hanger tube. Arrange film canisters or pill canisters below the pendulum. Show the children how to swing the pendulum to knock down the canisters. Discuss the movement of the pendulum. *Can you control its direction?*

Writing

❍ Print *wagon* on large index cards. Provide a sewing tool called a tracing wheel and invite the children to roll it over the letters.

❍ Print "Bumping ___ and ____ in my little red wagon" on a sheet of paper. Draw up and down arrows in the blanks. Give the children index cards with the words *up* and *down* on them. Challenge the children to place the correct word in the blank spot in the sentence. Prepare additional activities using other sentences from the song: "Swaying ____ to ____ in my little red wagon" and "Rocking ____ and ____ in my little red wagon."

Home Connection

❍ Encourage children to ask their families if they have used a wagon and why, and if they have ever ridden in a wagon. What was it like to ride in a wagon?

Down by the Station

Vocabulary

engine driver
puff
puffer-bellies
throttle
toot

Theme Connections

Community Workers
Sounds
Travel

Down by the station
Early in the morning,
See the little puffer-bellies
All in a row.
See the engine driver
Pull the little throttle.
Puff, puff! Toot, toot!
Off we go!

Did You Know?

○ In rail transport, a train consists of a single or several connected rail vehicles that are capable of being moved together along a track (guideway) to transport freight or passengers from one place to another. The track usually consists of conventional two-rail tracks, but may be monorail or maglev (magnetic levitation). Propulsion for the train may come from a variety of sources, but most often from a locomotive or self-propelled multiple unit (engine).

○ In railway terminology, a *consist* is used to describe the group of rail vehicles which make up a train.

○ A train can be a locomotive and attached cars, or be self-propelled. Trains can also be hauled by horses, pulled by a cable, or run downhill by gravity.

○ See pages 58 and 69 for more information about trains.

Literacy Links

Comprehension

○ Teach the children some of the fingerplays and action rhymes about trains (pages 95-96).

Oral Language

○ Discuss the words in the song that may be new vocabulary for the children. *What is a puffer-belly? Where is the throttle?*

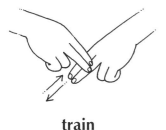

train

○ Discuss trains. *How are freight trains different from passenger trains?*
○ Discuss language that pertains to the train station, such as *platform*, *ticket counter*, *terminal*, and so on.
○ Teach the children the American Sign Language sign for *train*.

Phonological Awareness

○ Discuss the sounds a train makes as it travels down the track. *What does a train whistle sound like?* Tell the children that words that imitate the sound they are describing are called *onomatopoeia*.

Curriculum Connections

Blocks

○ Suggest that the children make a train track with blocks. Prepare a crossing. Provide signage, commercial or homemade. Encourage the children to build a town around the tracks.

Construction

○ Cut construction paper into squares, circles, rectangles, and triangles. Invite the children to put the shapes together to create a train.

Dramatic Play

○ Line chairs up in sets of two. Provide tickets, an engineer hat, trays, and other props. Invite the children to play "train." Ask the children where they are going and why.

Field Trip

○ Visit a train station. Point out the location of ticket agents, platforms, passenger waiting areas, and so on.

Games

○ Select a child to be the engine. Have the group recite the rhyme below. At the end of each verse, the engine selects another car (child).

> *Little red train,*
> *Chugging down the track,*
> *First it goes down,*
> *Then it comes back*
> *Hooking on cars one by one.*

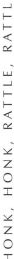

Listening

❍ Provide items that can be used to make a puffing sound such as empty squirt bottles and basters, or by puffing through paper towel tubes.

Math

❍ Photocopy and enlarge the Train Patterns (pages 112-113). Make one copy of the engine and caboose and ten copies of the passenger car. Print the numerals one through ten on the passenger cars. Use fewer cars or use dots on the cars for younger children. Encourage the children to place the cars behind the engine in numerical order.

Snack

❍ Invite the children to use the Marshmallow Trains Rebus Card (page 100) to make their snack. **Allergy Alert:** Check for peanut allergies.

Use pretzel sticks to hook the marshmallows together to create train cars.

 English Language Learner Strategy: Using a rebus makes it easier for English language learners to follow the directions.

❍ See pages 70-71 in "Little Red Caboose," pages 82-84 in "The Train," and pages 31-33 in "Clickety, Clack" for additional train activities.

Home Connections

❍ Encourage families to talk about places that they would like to visit by train.
❍ If possible, suggest that the children ask their families to watch a train pass along the tracks. They might discuss where they think the train is heading, what it contains, and how many cars the engine is pulling.

Book Corner

Down by the Station by Will Hillenbrand
The Little Engine That Could by Watty Piper
Train Song by Diane Siebert

 Special Needs Adaptation: Children with special needs who have experienced difficulty with completing or learning a new task often lack the self-confidence to keep trying. Read *The Little Engine That Could*. Explain that the engine kept trying even though it was difficult. Talk about things that are difficult for the child (tying his shoes, making new friends, sharing toys, and so on). Encourage the child to give himself a positive message, for example, "I think I can share my toys."

SONGS AND ACTIVITIES

27

Buckle Up

(Tune: The Ants Go Marching)
We like to travel in our car,
Hurrah, hurrah.
A car can take us near or far,
Hurrah, hurrah.
We buckle up before we go,
Whether we're going fast or slow,
So we'll all be safe
While riding in our car!
We buckle up before we go,
Whether we're going fast or slow,
So we'll all be safe
While riding in our car!

Vocabulary

buckle
far
fast
hurrah
near
riding
safe
slow

Theme Connections

Health and Safety
Movement

Did You Know?

❍ Car safety is especially critical for young children. The safety measures built into cars are designed for adults. Safety features that could save an adult can actually hurt a child. For example, all children age 12 and under must ride in the back seat. This is especially the case if there are airbags in the front seat, as airbags are only designed to protect adults and may injure or kill children.

❍ Child safety locks prevent children from accidentally opening doors from inside the vehicle, even if the door is unlocked. When the safety lock is on, the door can be opened only from the outside.

❍ Babies, children over 1 year old and between 20 and 40 pounds, and young children who weigh less than 80 pounds (40 kg), are younger than 8, or are shorter than 4 feet 9 inches (1.4 m) all have individual car seat or safety seat requirements. Be sure children are in the car, booster, or safety seat that is appropriate for their age, height, and weight.

Literacy Links

Oral Language

❍ Discuss other words that one might substitute for *hurrah*, such as *yippee, bravo,* or *whoopee.* Ask children what they say when they are excited and happy. Sing the song using one of the new words.

❍ Discuss the pairs of opposites mentioned in the song: *near* and *far, fast* and *slow*.

Print Awareness

❍ Print the song on chart paper. Move your hand beneath the words as the children sing. Point out the left-to-right and top-to-bottom movement of your hand.

Curriculum Connections

Art

❍ Encourage the children to draw pictures of children riding in a car.

Discovery

❍ Provide an inclined plank and encourage the children to roll cars down the plank and then push their cars back up the plank. *Which direction results in the car moving quickly (fast)? Which direction results in the car moving more slowly (slow)?*

Dramatic Play

❍ Provide open boxes large enough for children to sit in. Encourage the children to use the boxes as pretend cars. Use wide ribbon as pretend seat belts.

Fine Motor

❍ Provide a variety of buckles for children to explore.

❍ Place a metal thumb tack in the bottom of a toy car or tape a large paper clip to the bottom of the car. Draw a race track on a sheet of stiff plastic or poster board. Attach a disk magnet to a tongue depressor. Instruct children to place the car on the track and hold the tongue depressor under the track. Show them how to move the tongue depressor to rack the car around the track. Talk about race car drivers. Discuss the safety measures they use, including the use of a seat belt and harness.

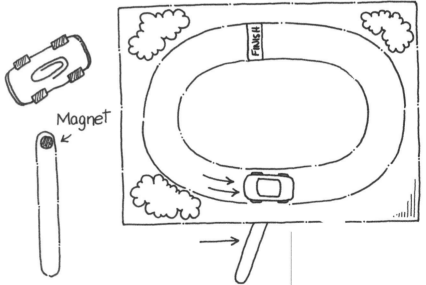

Magnet

Book Corner

Down by the Station by Will Hillenbrand

The Little Engine That Could by Watty Piper

Train Song by Diane Siebert

Listening

❍ Record car noises. For example, you might record a horn honking, a door shutting, a motor running, a seat belt snapping, and a radio playing. Provide a cassette player. Encourage the children to identify the sounds.

Special Event

❍ Invite a police officer to visit the school to discuss car safety. The police often have practice seat belts—be sure to ask if your visitor has access to a practice belt.

> **Special Needs Adaptation:** In addition to learning how to ride safely in a car, children with special needs may need additional instruction on how to cross the street safely. Practice crossing the street with the children. Use the following hand motions: Stop (hold out your hand palm upward), look (place your hand palm downward on your brow) and listen (cup your hand over your ear). Teach the following jingle to help children remember the rules: "Stop, look, and listen when you cross the street. Look to the left, then to right before you move your feet."

Writing

❍ Invite the children to make reminder signs for their cars. Print *Buckle Up* on chart paper. Provide drawing paper and writing utensils. Encourage the children to copy the words and then decorate their signs.

Home Connection

❍ Encourage children to ask family members to help them count the seat belts in their cars.

Clickety Clack

Vocabulary

big	springs
black	railroad
blow	track
engine	rattle
engineer	roll
freight cars	screech
jiggle	speeds
mattress	wave

Theme Connections

Community Workers
Sounds
Spatial Relationships

(Tune: Mary Had a Little Lamb)
Clickity, clickity, clickity clack!
The train speeds over the railroad track.
It rolls and rattles and screeches its song
And pulls and jiggles its
Freight cars along.

Clickity, clickity, clickity, clack!
The engine in front is big and black.
The cars are filled with lots of things
Like milk, or oil, or mattress springs.

Clickity, clickity, clickity, clack!
The engineer waves, and I wave back.
I count the cars as the freight train goes
And the whistle blows and blows...
And blows!

Did You Know?

○ Freight trains consist of wagons or trucks rather than carriages, although some parcel and mail trains (especially traveling post offices) look more like passenger trains. Traveling post offices were trains that had workers who sorted the mail while enroute. These were widely used in Europe until 2004. The last traveling post office ran on 9/1/2004.

○ In the United Kingdom, a train hauled by two locomotives is said to be "double-headed." In Canada and the United States, it is quite common for a long freight train to be headed by three, four, or even five locomotives.

○ Trains can also be mixed, hauling both passengers and freight. Such mixed trains have become rare in many countries, but were commonplace on the first 19th century railroads.

○ See pages 25 and 69 for more information about trains.

Literacy Links

Comprehension

○ Teach the children songs and rhymes (pages 94-96) about trains.

Oral Language

❍ Say a train-related sentence; for example, "I like trains." Challenge a child to add to your sentence; for example, "I like yellow trains." Select a second child and challenge her to add more to the sentence, for example, "I like yellow trains that carry passengers." Continue adding to the sentence until it becomes impossible to remember it all.

❍ Teach the children the American Sign Language sign for *train* (page 121).

Phonological Awareness

❍ Challenge the children to think of as many words as possible that rhyme with *train*. List their words on chart paper.

❍ Point out the *onomatopoeic* words (words that imitate the sound they are describing) in the song. *What other sound might a train make on the railroad track? What sound does the whistle make when it blows?*

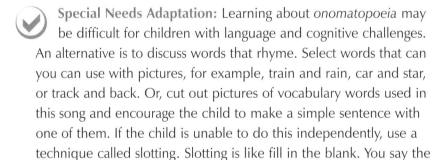 **Special Needs Adaptation:** Learning about *onomatopoeia* may be difficult for children with language and cognitive challenges. An alternative is to discuss words that rhyme. Select words that can you can use with pictures, for example, train and rain, car and star, or track and back. Or, cut out pictures of vocabulary words used in this song and encourage the child to make a simple sentence with one of them. If the child is unable to do this independently, use a technique called slotting. Slotting is like fill in the blank. You say the first part of a sentence and the child fills in the rest of the sentence.

Segmentation

❍ Invite the children to clap the syllables of the words, "clickity, clackity, clickity, clack!" *Which word has the fewest syllables?*

Curriculum Connections

Construction

❍ Have children paint and decorate shoeboxes. Cut out wheels from poster board or cardboard. Glue two wheels to each side of the shoeboxes.

Discovery

❍ Provide photos of a variety of different types of trains. Encourage the children to locate the trains that might be carrying passengers.

Gross Motor

○ Make tunnels by cutting the sides out of large boxes. Encourage the children to crawl through the tunnels while pretending to be a train.

Language

○ Trace the Train Patterns (pages 112-113) onto Pelon and color them with crayons. Give the train cars and a felt board to the children. Challenge them to make up a story about a train.

Math

○ Photocopy and enlarge the Train Patterns (pages 112-113). Make one copy of the engine and caboose and ten copies of the freight car. Print the numerals one through ten on the freight cars. Use fewer cars or use dots on the cars for younger children. Encourage the children to place the cars behind the engine in numerical order.

Snack

○ Invite the children to make a Graham Train as a snack. Take a rectangular piece of graham cracker and use cream cheese or peanut butter to add "wheels," such as dried apple rounds, round crackers, or banana slices. **Allergy Alert:** Check for peanut allergies.

Social Studies

○ Show the children a map. Point out how train tracks are represented on a map. Discuss the path of the tracks. *Where do they start and where do they end? Where might you travel on the train?*

Home Connection

○ Encourage children to ask a family member to help them find things in their homes that might have been transported by a freight train. Some examples are furniture, appliances, and even the family car.

All Aboard Trains by Mary Harding
Freight Train by Donald Crews
I Love Trains! by Philemon Sturges
Trains by Byron Barton

Crocodile Song

She sailed away on a
Happy summer day
On the back of a crocodile.
"You see," said she,
"He's as tame as he can be;
I'll ride him down the Nile."
Well, the croc winked his eye
As she waved them all goodbye,
Wearing a happy smile.
At the end of the ride
The lady was inside,
And the smile was on the
    crocodile!

✓ **Special Needs Adaptation:** Children with autism, especially those with the milder form known as Asperger's syndrome, may have difficulty with this song. Explain that is a pretend song and that the lady in the song was not hurt. Use the words *pretend*, *make-believe*, and *not real*.

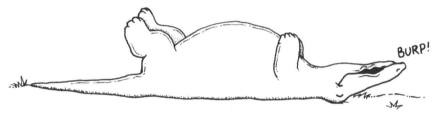
BURP!

Vocabulary

back
croc
crocodile
eye
happy
Nile (River)
ride
sailed
smile
tame
winked

Theme Connections

Animals
Seasons

Did You Know?

○ Crocodiles evolved about 200 million years ago from the Archosaurs. They lived at the same time as the dinosaurs and probably even ate them!
○ Crocodiles are reptiles that live both on land and in water. Like other reptiles, they breathe air.
○ Crocodiles can live to be 70-100 years old.
○ Crocodiles are "cold-blooded." To get warm, they lie in the sun. To cool down, they lie in the shade with their mouths wide open or laze in the water.
○ Crocodiles have the most highly developed brains of all reptiles.

Literacy Links

Comprehension

○ Say the rhyme "Three Little Monkeys" (page 96). Encourage the children to act out the rhyme.

Oral Language

○ Discuss the differences between crocodiles and alligators. Display a photo of each if available.

○ Demonstrate winking and blinking. Ask children to describe the difference. *When is winking used? When is blinking used?*

○ Teach the children American Sign Language sign for *goodbye.*

goodbye

Phonological Awareness

○ Ask the children what word in the song rhymes with Nile. *What word rhymes with "ride"?*

Print Awareness

○ Print *crocodile* and *croc* on chart paper. Explain that croc is a nickname for crocodile. Discuss nicknames. Do any of the children have nicknames?

Curriculum Connections

Construction

○ Invite the children to create crocodiles. Provide each child with a spring-action clothespin that has been painted green (use spray enamel away from the children). Give the children small wiggle eyes to glue to the top of the clothespin and a small piece of red felt to be glued inside the clothespin to represent a tongue. Provide white fabric pens for them to draw teeth, if desired.

Discovery

○ Show the children photographs of crocodiles. Point out the crocodile's feet. Discuss how their webbed feet allow them to swim easily. Show children a swimmer's fin and point out that fins are fashioned after the feet of animals that swim. Provide pictures of a variety of animals. Encourage the children to sort the animals by those that have webbed feet and those that do not.

 Special Needs Adaptation: Gather pictures of other animals with webbed feet and point out the similarities.

Dramatic Play

○ Place a green sheet over a rectangular table to create a crocodile. For added drama, make a crocodile head and tail from boxes. Encourage the children to pretend to be crocodiles.

Book Corner

Language

○ Discuss the texture of the crocodile's skin. Place a variety of textures of cloth including artificial alligator skin in a feely box. Challenge children to reach inside the box and locate the piece of cloth that feels like crocodile skin.

Social Studies

○ Show the children a globe and point out the location of the Nile River. *Where is the river? Do crocodiles really live in the river?*

Water Play

○ Provide plastic crocodiles and a water table or a dishpan of water for the children's play.

Writing

○ Print *crocodile* on a sheet of paper, leaving two blank spots for the letter "o" (cr_c_dile). Provide magnetic letters. Encourage the children to fill in the missing letters.

Home Connection

○ Encourage children to talk with their families about what they have learned about crocodiles and alligators.

Jingle Bells

Vocabulary

bright
dashing
fields
jingle
one-horse
open sleigh
sleighing song
spirits

Theme Connections

Holidays
Sounds

Jingle bells! Jingle bells!
Jingle all the way.
Oh, what fun it is to ride
In a one-horse open sleigh. Hey!
Jingle bells! Jingle bells!
Jingle all the way.
Oh, what fun it is to ride
In a one-horse open sleigh.

Dashing through the snow
In a one-horse open sleigh
O'er the fields we go
Laughing all the way. (Ha, ha, ha!)

Bells on bobtails ring,
Making spirits bright.
What fun it is to ride and sing
A sleighing song tonight!

Jingle bells! Jingle bells!
Jingle all the way.
Oh, what fun it is to ride
In a one-horse open sleigh. Hey!
Jingle bells! Jingle bells!
Jingle all the way.
Oh, what fun it is to ride
In a one-horse open sleigh.
Oh, what fun it is to ride
In a one-horse open sleigh.

Did You Know?

❍ "Jingle Bells" was written in 1850 by James Pierpont in Medford, Massachusetts (seven miles from Boston, Massachusetts). It was written as a celebration of the Salem Street sleigh races that were a popular recreation and porch-side spectator sport. Young people sang it on sleigh rides all winter long that year in the Medford area.

❍ In December 1857, Pierpont's brother asked if he knew of a pleasant winter song the Sunday school children could sing at a church social they were planning. James had stored the song in an attic trunk. He dusted off the only copy of the song that he had written years earlier in Medford and gave it to his brother. The children loved the song. It was a big hit of the Christmas social a few weeks later. Two years later in 1859 the song was officially published, and "Jingle Bells" has been a big hit ever since.

Literacy Links

Letter Knowledge

❍ Print *jingle bells* on index cards. Provide magnetic letters and encourage the children to copy the words.

Listening

❍ Have the children stand up and sit back down every time they hear the word "jingle" in the song.

Oral Language

❍ Discuss the unusual phrases in the song, "making spirits bright," "sleighing song," and "bob tails."

❍ Teach the children how to sing the following Spanish words to the tune of "Jingle Bells."

Casa belles

Casa belles, casa belles,
Hoy es Navidad.
Es un dia de algreia y felizidad.

Phonological Awareness

❍ Discuss different words used to describe laughter such as, *hee-hee, ha-ha,* and *ho-ho-ho*. Try using other laughing words in the song. Explain that the words that are used to describe the sound of laughter are called *onomatopoeic* words.

Curriculum Connections

Construction

❍ Invite the children to make sleighs. Provide flat boxes, paint, and yarn. Attach the yarn as a handle to one end of the box. Encourage children to decorate their sleighs and then pull dolls or stuffed animals across the floor in their sleighs.

Discovery

❍ Freeze a pie tin or cake pan of water. Allow children to tilt the pan slightly and then explore sliding items such as buttons, washers, blocks, cotton balls, pompoms, and so on over the ice. *Which items move more easily?*

❍ Create an inclined plank. Provide items with wheels and without wheels for children to roll or slide down the plank. *Which items move more quickly?*

Book Corner

Jingle Bell Mice by
    Lisa McCue
Jingle Bells by
    Carolyn Ewing
Jingle Bells by Iza
    Trapani

Fine Motor

- Make Snow Dough. Mix 1 cup flour, ½ cup salt, 1 cup water, 2 tablespoons vegetable oil, 1 tablespoon cream tartar, ⅓ cup clear glitter, and ¼ cup powdered white tempera paint. Cook over medium heat, stirring until a ball is formed. Let cool a bit and then knead dough until it is cool. Invite the children to fashion the dough as desired. *Does the dough look like snow? Does it feel like snow?*
- Provide jingle bells and yarn. Invite the children to string the bells. If desired, show them how to tie a knot after each bell is strung so that they can create a string of bells.

>  **Special Needs Adaptation:** For children with less developed motor skills, use larger bells or dip the string or yarn in glue and let it dry before the child starts to string the bells. It will stiffen the yarn or string so that the bells can go on more easily.

Gross Motor

- Invite the children to take off their shoes and slide across a tile or hardwood floor surface in thier socks. **Safety Warning:** Supervise closely.

Listening

- Provide bells and a variety of containers such as margarine tins, coffee cans, plastic jars, and other containers. Encourage the children to place bells in different types of containers and explore the resulting sounds. *Which containers increase the sound of the bells?*

Math

- Place two bells in one blue envelope and three bells in a second blue envelope. Place three bells in one yellow envelope and five bells in a second yellow envelope. Continue placing uneven sets of bells in pairs of colored envelopes. Encourage the children to examine the sound of each pair of envelopes to determine which envelope has the most bells inside.

Music and Movement

- Play classical music and invite the children to dance with a shaker of jingle bells in their hands or with the string of jingle bells they strung.

Home Connection

- Encourage the children to sing "Jingle Bells" with their families. Have the children ask their family members if they can remember who taught them the song, "Jingle Bells."

Walk, Walk, Walk Your Feet

by Pam Schiller and Richele Bartkowiak

(Tune: Row, Row, Row Your Boat)
Walk, walk, walk your feet
Everywhere you go.
Walk 'em fast, walk 'em slow,
Walk them heel to toe.

Tap, tap, tap your toes
Tap 'em to the beat.
Tap 'em fast, tap 'em slow,
Rock your little feet.

Clap, clap, clap your hands,
Clap them high and low.
Clap 'em fast, clap 'em slow,
No matter where you go.

Sing, sing, sing this song,
Sing it loud and clear.
Sing it fast, sing it slow
Fill your heart with cheer.

Vocabulary

beat
cheer
clap
clear
fast
feet
high
loud
low
rock
sing
slow
tap
toes
walk

Theme Connections

Movement
Parts of the Body

Did You Know?

❍ One quarter of all the bones in the human body are found in the feet.

❍ Left-handed people are generally left-footed as well. They put their left foot forward first when they walk.

❍ Walking is one of the simplest aerobic exercises you can do. It will help you strengthen your bones, control your weight, and condition your heart and lungs.

❍ Being consistent in a walking exercise routine is one of the most important factors in developing a healthy physical activity program. Research has shown that people who walk approximately 20-25 miles per week outlive those who don't walk by several years. On average, every minute of walking can extend your life by one and a half to two minutes. That's about a two-for-one trade-off!

❍ Walking an extra 20 minutes each day will burn off seven pounds of body fat per year.

❍ See page 91 in "Put Your Little Foot" for more information about feet and walking.

Literacy Links

Listening
❍ Have the children touch their feet each time they hear the word "feet" in the song.

Oral Language
❍ Discuss words that are synonyms for *slow*. Do the same thing for *fast*.
❍ Teach the children the American Sign Language signs for *feet*, *fast*, and *slow* (page 121).

Print Awareness
❍ Print the words to the song on chart paper. Move your hand under the words as the children sing them. Point out the direction of the print—top to bottom and left to right.

Curriculum Connections

Art
❍ Provide drawing paper, a shallow tub of tempera paint, and a tub of clean soapy water and a towel. Encourage the children to take off their shoes and socks and step first into the paint and then onto their paper. After the footprints dry, encourage the children to look at them closely. Provide a magnifying glass for a better look. Challenge children to think of something they can make from their foot prints.

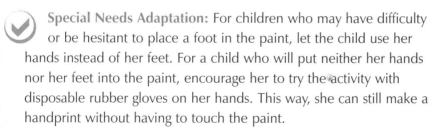 **Special Needs Adaptation:** For children who may have difficulty or be hesitant to place a foot in the paint, let the child use her hands instead of her feet. For a child who will put neither her hands nor her feet into the paint, encourage her to try the activity with disposable rubber gloves on her hands. This way, she can still make a handprint without having to touch the paint.

Field Trip
❍ Take a walking field trip outside around the building, around the block, or to a specific destination. Alternate walking with skipping, galloping, or tiptoeing.

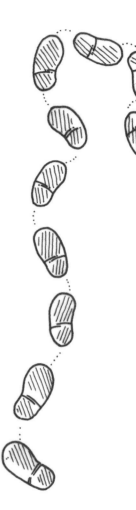

Book Corner

The Listening Walk by Paul Showers

Mama Went Walking by Christine Berry

On My Way to Buy Eggs by Chih-Yuan Chen

Rosie's Walk by Pat Hutchins

Fine Motor

○ Place stringing beads in a shallow tub. Sit a small chair beside the tub. Invite the children to take off their shoes, sit in the chair, and try to pick up the beads with their toes.

Games

○ Play Red Light, Green Light. Select one person to be the "stoplight." Have the "stoplight" stand at one end of the playground and all the other children form a line about 15 feet away. The stoplight faces away from the line of children and says, "Green light." At this point the children are allowed to move towards the stoplight. At any point, the stoplight may say, "Red light!" and turn around. If any of the children are caught moving when the stoplight turns around, they must return to the start line. Play resumes when the stoplight turns back around and says "green light." The first player to touch the stoplight becomes the next stoplight.

Gross Motor

○ Use masking tape to make a zigzag line on the floor. Invite the children to walk the line heel to toe and then toe to heel.

Math

○ Encourage the children to remove their shoes and find someone who has a foot that is smaller than their foot and someone who has a foot that is larger than their foot.

○ Have the children walk around the perimeter of the room or playground counting their steps. Have them take baby steps the first time. Have them take giant steps the second time. *Which type of step requires them to count to a higher number?*

Writing

○ Write *foot* and *feet* on drawing paper. Provide magnetic letters and encourage the children to copy the words. Talk with them as they work. *Which letters are different in the words?*

Home Connection

○ Encourage the children to invite their families to take a family walk.

Little Canoe

Vocabulary

around	moon
boy	paddling
canoe	shining
dim	sound
dipped	swim
girl	swimming
kiss	

Theme Connections

Friends and Families
Nighttime

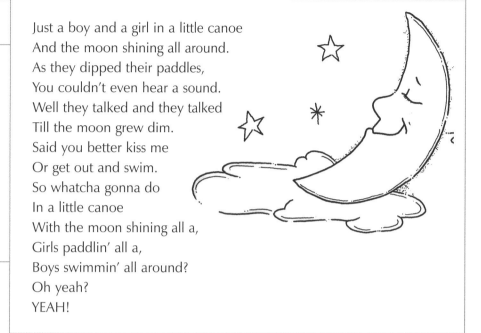

Just a boy and a girl in a little canoe
And the moon shining all around.
As they dipped their paddles,
You couldn't even hear a sound.
Well they talked and they talked
Till the moon grew dim.
Said you better kiss me
Or get out and swim.
So whatcha gonna do
In a little canoe
With the moon shining all a,
Girls paddlin' all a,
Boys swimmin' all around?
Oh yeah?
YEAH!

Did You Know?

❍ A canoe is a relatively small human-powered boat. Canoes are pointed at both ends and usually open on top.
❍ Canoes are propelled by the use of paddles, with the number of paddlers depending on the size of canoe.
❍ Paddlers face in the direction of travel, either seated on supports in the hull, or kneeling directly upon the hull. In this way, paddling a canoe can be contrasted with rowing, where the rowers face away from the direction of travel. Paddles may be single-bladed or double-bladed.
❍ Canoes were the primary form of travel for several tribes of American Indians, including the Algonquin and the Cree.

Literacy Links

Oral Language

❍ Show the children photographs of rowboats and canoes. Discuss the similarities and differences of canoes and rowboats. Make a list of the things that both boats have in common. *Have you ever been in a canoe or a rowboat?*
❍ Teach the children the American Sign Language signs for *girl* (page 121) and *boy* (page 120).

Phonological Awareness
○ Help the children make a list of words that rhyme with *canoe*.

Curriculum Connections

Art
○ Provide paper and markers or crayons. Suggest that the children draw a canoe.

Construction
○ Provide paper plates, yarn, wiggle eyes, markers, craft sticks, and other materials. Invite each child to make a girl and a boy puppet using paper plates and craft sticks. Have them use construction paper or markers to add facial features to the plates.
○ Invite the children to make canoes. Fold a piece of 9" x 12" construction paper in half length-wise. About a half-inch from the fold line make another fold. Do this on both sides of the original fold. The paper should now look like a capital "W." The folds will be the bottom of the canoe. Draw a canoe shape on the paper (make sure the folds are on the bottom of the canoe). Cut the canoe shape and punch a few holes on each end. Use yarn to weave through the holes. Push the folded floor of the canoe flat so that the canoe sits.

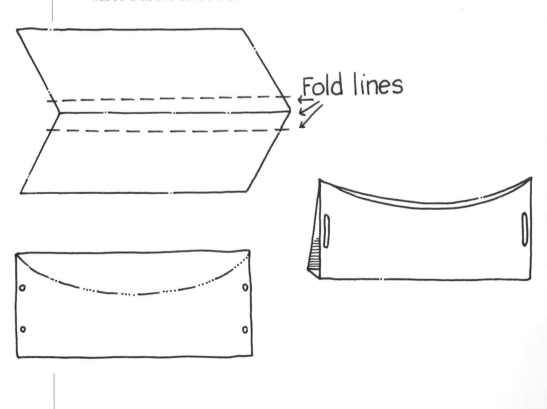

Fold lines

Book Corner

Canoe Days by Gary Paulsen
Little Red Fox and His Canoe by Nathaniel Benchley
Three Days on a River in a Red Canoe by Vera B. Williams

✓ **Special Needs Adaptation:** To encourage cooperative play, place several carpet squares together or draw a canoe on large paper. Tell the children that it is a pretend canoe. Ask children to take turns sitting in the canoe and paddling across the lake. To add to the effect, lay a large blue bed sheet across the floor, and pretend that it is the water. Place the carpet squares (the "canoe") on the sheet. For a child who may be unwilling or unable to paddle, assign him the job of lookout. The lookout watches the water for obstacles that may be in the path of the canoe.

Discovery/Math
❍ Provide a tub of water and items from the classroom, such as plastic interlocking blocks, teddy bear counters, erasers, wooden blocks, plastic cups and utensils, and other items that might sink or float. Suggest that the children test each item for its ability to float. Ask children to sort the items by those that float and those that sink.

Dramatic Play
❍ Provide a light source such as a lamp, flashlight, or overhead projector. Encourage the children to imagine what moonlight shadows would look like and then make them.

Language
❍ Provide a basket of items in which some of the items rhyme with *canoe*; for example, blue paper, numeral two, and a shoe. Encourage the children to sort the items into things that rhyme with *canoe* and things that don't.

Water Play
❍ Provide craft sticks for paddles and challenge the children to move the water in the water table without making a splash.

Writing
❍ Print *boy* and *girl* on index cards. Provide fingerpaint and encourage the children make fingerprints over the letters.

Home Connection

❍ Encourage the children to ask their families what they know about canoes and how to paddle them.

Barges

Out of my window, looking in the night
I can see the barges' flickering light.
Silently flows the river to the sea
And the barges too go silently.

Chorus:
Barges, I would like to go with you.
I would like to sail the ocean blue.
Barges, have you treasures in your hold?
Do you fight with pirates brave and bold?

Out of my window, looking in the night
I can see the barges' flickering light.
Starboard shines green and port is glowing red.
I can see them flickering far ahead.

(Chorus)

Vocabulary

ahead	pirates
barges	port
blue	red
flickering	sail
flows	silently
green	starboard
light	treasures
night	window
ocean	

Theme Connections

Colors
Nighttime

Did You Know?

❍ A barge is a flat-bottomed boat, built mainly for river and canal transport of heavy goods.

❍ Most barges are not self-propelled and need to be towed or pushed by tugboats.

❍ Barges on canals (towed by draft animals on an adjacent towpath) competed with railroads in the mid-nineteenth century. Barges lost because railroads had higher speeds, lower costs, and more routes.

❍ Barges are still used today for bulk items, because the cost of hauling goods by barge is very low.

❍ There are a variety of barges: barrack barges (living quarters), dry bulk cargo barges (rock and grain), liquid cargo barges (water, petroleum, and other liquids), railcar barges (special rigs for loading), and royal barges (ceremonial).

Literacy Links

Oral Language
❍ Discuss the differences between barges and cruise ships.

❍ Define *starboard* and *port* as they pertain to a ship or boat. Starboard is the nautical term (used on boats and ships) that refers to the right side of a vessel, as perceived by a person facing the direction of travel. Port is the nautical term (used on boats and ships) that refers to the left side of a ship, as perceived by a person facing forward, towards the bow (the front of the vessel). A port is also a facility at the edge of an ocean, river, or lake for receiving ships and transferring cargo and persons to them. Ports have specially-designed equipment to help in the loading and unloading of these vessels.

Phonological Awareness
❍ Invite the children to help find the rhyming words in the song. *Which word rhymes with night? Which word rhymes with blue?*

Curriculum Connections

Blocks
❍ Place blue bulletin board paper or a blue sheet on the floor to represent a river or an ocean. Invite the children to build a town around the water. Provide shoebox lids to use for barges. Encourage the children to use the "barges" to move things like cars or blocks across the water.

Discovery
❍ Provide a light source such as a flashlight. Show the children how to pass a sheet of paper or a block in front of the light to make the light flicker. *What causes the lights to appear as if they are flickering from the barges?* Challenge the children to apply this concept to barges floating down a river passing behind trees or other vessels on the water.
❍ Provide a tub filled half full with water, a Styrofoam meat tray, and blocks. Use a strip of masking tape to mark the water level in the tub. Place the Styrofoam meat tray in the tub. Place one block on the tray. *What happens to the water level?* Place a second block on the tray. *What happens?* Help the children predict what will happen when a third block is placed on the barge. Tell the children that the term that describes the relationship between water level and weight is called displacement.

Fine Motor
❍ Glue a strip of magnetic tape to the bottom of a Styrofoam meat tray. Paint the bottom of a shallow box blue to represent the ocean. Place the Styrofoam meat tray (the barge) in the shallow box. Show the children how to move the barge (meat tray) across the ocean by moving a magnet under the box. (See illustration on next page.)

Book Corner

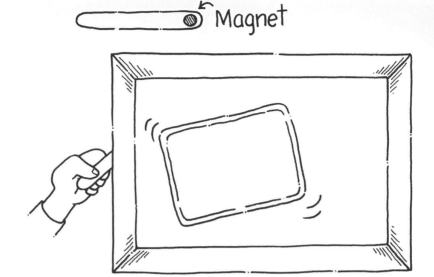

Games

❍ Invite the childre to participate in a treasure hunt. (Use the Treasure Hunt on page 119.) Decide what the treasure will be, such as a snack or a special book you will read. Read the first card to the children, and let them find the next clue using the rebus hints. Continue until the children find the "treasure."

Sand Table

❍ Hide treasure (pennies) in the sand table. Challenge the children to find the treasure.

Water Play

❍ Give the children Styrofoam meat trays to use as barges. Provide blocks, cars, and other items for the barges to carry.

> ✔ **Special Needs Adaptation:** For children with limited motor skills, use square Styrofoam plates (use the kind with several different divided areas for food). It will be easier for items to "ride" in each food compartment. Another adaptation is to provide a large tongue depressor for the child to use to help guide his barge across the water.

Home Connection

❍ Encourage children to talk with their families about barges. *Have they ever seen a barge? Where? What was the barge carrying?*

White Wings

Vocabulary

arrow	sea
cheerily	straight
cliffs	weary
craggy	white
night	wing
sail	yacht

Theme Connections

Colors
Nighttime
Weather

White wings they never grow
    weary,
They cheerily carry me over
    the sea.
Night falls, I long for thee dearie,
I lift up my white wings and sail
    home to thee.

Sail home, as straight as an arrow,
My yacht shoots along on the
    crest of the sea.
Sail home, to sweet Maggie
    Darrow,
In her dear little home she is
    waiting for me.

High up where cliffs they are
    craggy
There's where the girl of my
    heart waits for me.
Heigh ho, I long for you, Maggie.
I'll lift up my white wings and sail
    home to thee.

White wings they never grow
    weary,
They carry me cheerily over
    the sea.
Night falls, I long for my dearie,
I'll lift up my white wings and sail
    home to thee.
I'll lift up my white wings and sail
    home to thee.

Did You Know?

○ A sailing ship is a wind-powered ship. Historically, sailing ships were the primary means of transportation across large bodies of water, such as lakes, and oceans, before the invention of workable steam engines.

○ A sailing ship was used for carrying cargo, passengers, mail, supplies, and other essential items. In modern times, sailing ships are less common but are still used as commercial vessels in some parts of the world, such as the Indian Ocean.

○ Small sailing boats are still used for fishing in developing countries and for recreational purposes in many countries. There are also many tall ship training vessels that provide recreational sailing.

Literacy Links

Letter Knowledge

○ Print *white wings* on chart paper. Ask the children to identify the first letter in each word. Are there any other letters that are in both words?

Oral Language

○ Discuss sailboats. *How are sailboats like rowboats? How are they different?*

○ Ask the children why they think the writer of the song refers to boat sails as wings. You may want to tell the children that when a writer lets one thing stand for another he or she is using a figure of speech called a *metaphor*.

○ Teach the children the American Sign Language sign for *sailboat* (page 121).

Phonological Awareness

○ Print *sailboat* on chart paper. Draw a line between the words *sail* and *boat*. Tell the children that *sailboat* is a *compound word*. Compound words are words that are made up of two words. Help the children make a list of other compound words they know; for example, *doghouse*, *popcorn*, and *football*.

Curriculum Connections

Construction

○ Invite the children to make sailboats. Cut a triangle from a piece of construction paper to make a sail. Invite the children to decorate their sails with crayons, markers, and/or stickers. Punch three holes along one side of the triangle (sail). Weave a straw through the holes to create a mast. Place a ball of clay in the middle of a three-inch plastic lid and then press the mast (straw) into the clay. Provide a tub of water for children to sail their boats.

Discovery

○ Provide paper plates to use as wings. Encourage the children to use their wings to fan a feather across the floor.

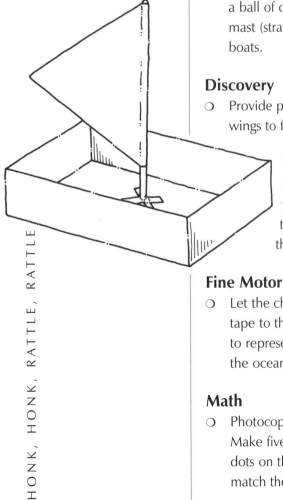

Dramatic Play

○ Build a sailboat for children to use for dramatic play. Cut a triangular sail from bulletin board paper to create a sail. Use duct tape to secure the sail to a dowel or a broom handle (mast). Tape the mast and sail to a large box to create a sailboat.

Fine Motor

○ Let the children make sailboats (see Construction). Glue a strip of magnetic tape to the bottom of the sailboats. Paint the bottom of a shallow box blue to represent the ocean. Show the children how to move the sailboat across the ocean by moving a magnet under the box.

Math

○ Photocopy and enlarge the sail and Sailboat Patterns (pages 110-111). Make five copies. Place the numerals 1-5 on the sails and place one to five dots on the boats. Laminate the boats and sails. Encourage the children to match the sails to the boats.

The Boat Alphabet Book by Jerry Pallotta
The Boat Book by Gail Gibbons
The Little Sailboat by Lois Lenski

Music and Movement
❍ Provide white streamers and encourage the children to dance with the streamers to classical music. Suggest that they pretend they are sails blowing in the wind.

Outdoors
❍ Provide a parachute or large sheet. Have the children gather around it. Show them how to toss the sheet into the air without letting go and then allow it to drift down.
❍ Blow bubbles and encourage the children to keep the bubbles in the air by blowing on them or fanning them.

Science
❍ Provide a tub of water and items to test for their ability to sink or float. Encourage the children to sort the items first by predicting whether or not the item will sink or float and then have them test the items to see if they predicted correctly.

> **Special Needs Adaptation:** Wrap a sheet of white paper around two containers, such as coffee cans or plastic jars. Write *float* on one container and *sink* on the other. After a child has experimented with an object to see if will sink or float, invite her to take it out of the water and place it in the correct container based on whether it sank or floated.

Snack
❍ Make Sailboat Eggs. Hard boil some eggs (adult only step). Peel the eggs and rinse. Cut them in half. Remove the yolks from both halves of the eggs with a spoon. For each egg, mix the yolk with about one to 1 ½ teaspoon mayonnaise or salad dressing, ⅛ teaspoon mustard (about one squeeze), and ¼ teaspoon (about two squeezes) ketchup in a small bowl. Put the yolk mixture back into each egg half and place a toothpick into each half egg. Place raisins, marshmallows, or other small snack on the toothpick to create a sail.

Home Connection

❍ Suggest that children ask their families who (or what) they would like to sail away to see. Encourage children to tell their families who (or what) they would like to see.

A Sailor Went to Sea

A sailor went to sea, sea, sea
To see what he could see, see, see.
But all that he could see, see, see
Was the bottom of the deep blue
Sea, sea, sea!
(Repeat)

Vocabulary

blue
bottom
deep
sailor
sea
see

Theme Connections

Colors
Oceans
Travel

Did You Know?

❍ A *sailor* is a member of the crew of a ship or boat. The term may comprise anyone from an admiral in the navy to a person who goes out sailing on weekends as a hobby. *Sailor* is also used to describe an enlisted member of a naval force.

❍ In the minds of members of the United States Navy and the Royal Navy, *sailor* refers to someone who is under sail and not on a vessel with motorized power of any kind.

❍ In the Merchant Navy, *sailor* has often been used to distinguish able seamen, ordinary seamen, and other members of the deck crew from crew members working in other departments, such as catering and the engine room.

Literacy Links

Oral Language

❍ Print *sea* and *see* on chart paper. Read the words to the children. Define each word. Explain that sometimes words that have completely different meanings sound the same. These words are called *homophones*.

❍ Have the children say *sea*. Invite a volunteer to say a sentence with the word in it.

Phonological Awareness

❍ Encourage the children to brainstorm as many words that rhyme with *sea* as they can.

Segmentation

❍ Ask the children to clap the syllables in the words *sailor* and *sea*. *Which word has the most syllables?*

> **Special Needs Adaptation:** Sounding out and counting syllables is a very critical early literacy activity. If the child can not clap his hands in cadence with the syllables, provide a small drum or drum made from an oatmeal carton. Use a craft stick as a drum stick. Since practice is very important when learning a new skill, look for other opportunities for the child to clap, beat, or tap out the syllables to a word. Try using his name or the names of the food you will be eating. Be creative! The more the child practices, the easier it will be for him to grasp the concept of syllables.

Curriculum Connections

Art

❍ Provide several shades of blue paint and encourage the children to paint the ocean.

Construction

❍ Make a simple periscope. Clip a mirror to one end of a ruler. Show the children how to use the periscope to see around a corner. Discuss how periscopes are used on a submarine.

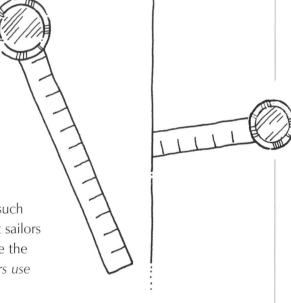

Discovery

❍ Provide vision-enhancing items, such as binoculars and sunglasses, that sailors use. Invite the children to explore the materials. *Why do you think sailors use these items?*

Book Corner

Henry the Sailor Cat
    by Henry
    Calhoun
I Saw a Ship a' Sailing
    by Mary Hay
The Sailor Dog by
    Margaret Wise
    Brown

Dramatic Play

❍ Provide sailor clothing and encourage the children to dress like sailors.

Fine Motor

❍ Provide a pail of soapy water and handheld beaters. Encourage the children to make sea foam by beating the soapy water.

Gross Motor

❍ Teach the children how to make a Wave movement. Have the children form a circle. Stand in the center of the circle and perform a movement, such as raising both hands over your head. Have the children copy the movement, in turn, around the circle. Invite volunteers to take a turn creating a movement. *Why is this called "The Wave?"*

Music and Movement

❍ Provide "sailing" music and encourage the children to rock to the music as if they were being tossed by the ocean waves.

Water Play

❍ Add blue food coloring to the water in the water play table. Provide toy boats for dramatic play.

Writing

❍ Provide a shallow tray of sand. Print *sailor* and *sea* on chart paper. Encourage the children to use their index fingers as a writing tool to copy the words in the sand.

❍ See pages 76-77 in "My Bonnie Lies Over the Ocean" for additional ocean activities.

Home Connection

❍ Suggest that children ask at home if they have any sailors in the family.

Alice the Camel

Vocabulary

camel
five
four
horse
humps
one
three
two

Theme Connections

Animals
Counting

Alice the camel has five humps.
Alice the camel has five humps.
Alice the camel has five humps.
So go, Alice, go.

Alice the camel has four humps.
Alice the camel has four humps.
Alice the camel has four humps.
So go, Alice, go.

Alice the camel has three humps.
Alice the camel has three humps.
Alice the camel has three humps.
So go, Alice, go.

Alice the camel has two humps.
Alice the camel has two humps.
Alice the camel has two humps.
So go, Alice, go.

Alice the camel has one hump.
Alice the camel has one hump.
Alice the camel has one hump.
So go, Alice, go.

Alice the camel has no humps.
Alice the camel has no humps.
Alice the camel has no humps.
Now Alice is a horse!

(The children stand as they sing the song. They hold up the correct number of fingers to correspond with each verse and bump hips with a friend on the words "go Alice, go.")

Did You Know?

❍ Camels are desert animals. Most of the animals that live in the desert are small, like beetles and lizards.

❍ A camel is fully grown when it is seven to eight years old. Camels can live for about 45 years.

❍ The camel's coat is thick to insulate against both heat and cold. The desert is very hot during the day, but gets very cold at night (almost freezing).

❍ Camels are able to go for some days without drinking water. The camel conserves water in its body cells and its stomach. Conserving means it doesn't excrete water through sweating or urinating.

❍ Camels have very long legs to keep their big bodies high off the hot ground. Even when a camel sits down its belly will not touch the ground. It has a pillow-like callus under its chest to balance it and make it comfortable to rest on the sand, even when it is hot. The camel has very hard skin on its knees to protect the knees when the camel rests on them.

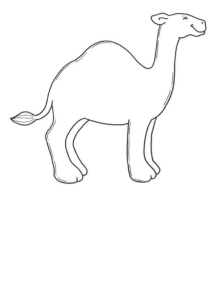

Literacy Links

Oral Language
❍ Discuss the differences between camels and horses.

Print Awareness
❍ Print *Go, Alice, Go* on chart paper. Provide magnetic letters and encourage the children to copy the phrase. Challenge children to substitute their own names for Alice's name.

Segmentation
❍ Clap the syllables in *Alice*. Clap the syllables in each child's name. Challenge the children to find a friend whose name has two syllables like Alice. Sing the song substituting the new name.

Curriculum Connections

Art
❍ Provide brown paint and encourage the children to paint a camel with as many humps as they would like.

Games
❍ Play Pin the Tail on the Camel. Photocopy and enlarge a camel from the Camel Patterns (pages 103-105). Color the camel. Remove the tail and laminate both the body and the tail. Place the camel's body on the wall. Put masking tape on the back side of the tail. Encourage the children to stand six feet away from the camel and, with their eyes closed, attempt to place the tail on the camel.
❍ Photocopy and enlarge four camels from the Camel Patterns (pages 103-105). Color and laminate the camels. Glue a strip of magnetic tape to the back of each camel. Provide each child with a 12" x 24" piece of yellow poster board to use as a game board. Draw a start line, a finish line, and a path in between on each board. Give each child a camel and a magnet and encourage them to race their camels from the start to the finish line by moving a magnet under the board.

Book Corner

The Camel's Lament by Charles Santore

How the Camel Got Its Hump by Justine Fontes

Pamela Camel by Bill Peet

Gross Motor

❍ Provide knee pads. Have the children try crawling across the floor without knee pads and then with knee pads. *Is it more comfortable to crawl with or without knee pads?* Remind the children that camels have pads on their knees for protection.

Math/Fine Motor

❍ Photocopy and enlarge the Camel Patterns on pages 103-105. Have the children arrange the camels by the number of humps on their back from least to most. Provide playdough and have the children make humps (round balls) to match the number of humps on the camels.

> **Special Needs Adaptation:** Modify by working with the child. Ask him to arrange the camels by the number of humps, or help him count the total number of camels or the number of humps on each camel's back. Write the number of humps on each camel's back on the camel. Encourage the child to take the camel home and count the humps with a family member.

Science

❍ Place photos of desert animals in the science center for children to observe. *Which is the largest animal in the group? Do any of the desert animals also live in other parts of the world?*

Snack

❍ Serve Camel Hump Sodas for snack. Add root beer flavoring to shaved ice and serve rounded scoops in paper cones. Add a straw and enjoy.

Home Connection

❍ Encourage the children to tell their families two camel facts. Perhaps they will share information about a camel's humps, or how a camel is different from a horse, or where camele live.

This Little Train

by Pam Schiller and Richele Bartkowiak

(Tune: This Old Man)
This little car, painted black
Zooming down the railroad track,
With a toot-toot, click-clack
Wind behind his back,
This little train is rockin' on.

This little car, painted blue
Has a seat for me and you,
With a toot-toot, click-clack
Wind behind his back,
This little train is rockin' on.

This little car, painted yellow
Carries the conductor, a mighty
fine fellow,
With a toot-toot, click-clack
Wind behind his back,
This little train is rockin' on.

This little car, painted green
Nicest car you've ever seen,
With a toot-toot, click-clack
Wind behind his back,
This little train is rockin' on.

This little car, painted grey
Will take you places far away,
With a toot-toot, click-clack
Wind behind his back,
This little train is rockin' on.

This caboose, painted red
Has four seats and one soft bed,
With a toot-toot, click-clack
Wind behind his back,
This little train is rockin' on.

Vocabulary

back	grey
bed	nicest
black	railroad
blue	seat
caboose	toot
clack	track
click	train
conductor	wind
fellow	yellow
fellow	zoom
green	zooming

Theme Connections

Colors
Sounds

Did You Know?

❍ A passenger train may have one or several locomotives, and one or more coaches. Alternatively, a train may be entirely passenger-carrying coaches, some or all of which are powered as a multiple unit. In many parts of the world, particularly Japan and Europe, high-speed rail is utilized extensively for passenger travel.

❍ High-speed rail is public transport by rail with a possible speed above 200 km/h (125 miles per hour). Typically, high-speed trains travel at top service speeds of between 150 mph (250 km/h) to 160 mph (300 km/h). Although the world speed record for a wheeled train was set in 1990 by a French high-speed train that reached a speed of 320 mph (515 km/h), the experimental Japanese magnetic levitation train has reached 361 mph (581 km/h).

❍ See pages xx and xx for more information about trains.

Literacy Links

Comprehension
❍ Teach the children fingerplays and action rhymes about trains (pages 95-96).

Oral Language
❍ Invite a volunteer to demonstrate what a *rockin'* train might look like.
❍ Discuss passenger trains. *Has anyone you know ever traveled by train? Where did they go? Have you ever traveled by train? If so, where did you go?*
❍ Teach the children the American Sign Language sign for *train* (page 121).
❍ Below is another song about colorful train cars. Teach it to the children and encourage them to name their favorite color for a train car.

> **Pretty Cars** (Tune: Twinkle, Twinkle, Little Star)
> *Blue cars, green cars, yellow, grey, and black*
> *And there's the red car bringing up the back.*
> *Blue cars, green cars, yellow, grey, and black.*
> *See the pretty train cars on the railroad track.*

Phonological Awareness
❍ Say each color word and ask the children to provide rhyming words that match the color word.
❍ Discuss the *onomatopoeic* words (words that imitate the sound they are describing) toot-toot and click-clack. *What other sounds might a train make?*

Print Awareness
❍ Show children signs that signal a train crossing.

Curriculum Connections

Blocks
❍ Demonstrate how to create train tracks on the floor using masking tape. Give the children masking tape and encourage them to create train tracks. Encourage them to use blocks for trains and buildings along the train tracks.

Construction

❍ Provide shoeboxes and encourage the children to use tempera paint to paint the boxes colors that correspond with the train cars mentioned in the song. Provide round black construction paper wheels and encourage the children to glue the wheels to each car. Suggest the children move each car along the track that the children in the block center have created.

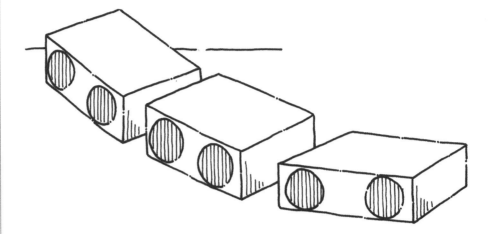

Dramatic Play

❍ Set up a bed and sitting area in a caboose. Encourage the children to take turns pretending they are the train conductors.

Language

❍ Photocopy the Color Word Rhyming Game (pages 114-115). Trace each color word with the appropriate color marker and then color the pictures. Cut and laminate the pages. Invite the children to match each picture to the color word it rhymes with.

Listening

❍ Give the children empty toilet paper towel tubes. Encourage the children to use the tubes as train whistles.

Math

❍ Photocopy and enlarge the train cars in the Train Patterns (pages 112-113.) Color the train cars to match the colors mentioned in the song. Draw dots on the train cars beginning with one dot and continuing with two dots on the next car, three on the next, and so on up to five dots. Laminate the train cars. Encourage the children to arrange the train cars from the least to the most dots.

Book Corner

Snack

❍ Invite the children to make colored train cars. Provide them with graham crackers that have been broken into small rectangles (¼ sections). Provide several different colors of icing. Provide a plastic knife for children to spread the icing of their choice onto their graham cracker. Add colored lifesaver candies for wheels.

Writing

❍ Print each of the color words mentioned in the song on index cards. Encourage the children to use crayons and tracing paper to trace over the words. Are they able to match the correct color of crayon to the color word?

> **Special Needs Adaptation:** As an alternative to writing or tracing the names of colors, collect four or five containers and cover the outside of each with white paper. Attach a paper square of a different color to each container. Gather objects from around the room and encourage the child to place each item into the appropriate color container. Talk about each color (for example, the color of trees, apples, and so on). Ask the child to show you something in the room that is red, blue, yellow, green, and so on. Use color words throughout the day to reinforce their meaning for children who may have language delays. An example might be to say, "All of the children who are wearing blue may wash their hands" or "All of the children who are wearing yellow may sit down."

❍ See pages 31-33 in "Clickety Clack," pages 25-27 in "Down by the Station," pages 82-84 in "The Train," and pages 70-71 in "The Little Red Caboose" for additional train activities.

Home Connection

❍ Encourage the children to bring an item from home that rhymes with *blue*.

A Bicycle Built for Two

Daisy, Daisy, give me your answer true.
I'm half crazy all for the love of you.
It won't be a stylish marriage.
I can't afford a carriage.
But you'll look sweet, upon the seat
Of a bicycle built for two.

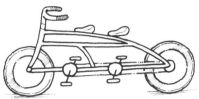

Vocabulary

afford
answer
bicycle built for two
carriage
crazy
love
marriage
seat
stylish
sweet
true

Theme Connections

Counting
Friends and Families

Did You Know?

○ When Harry Dacre, a popular English composer, first came to the United States, he brought with him a bicycle, for which he was charged duty (tax). His friend (the songwriter William Jerome) remarked lightly: "It's lucky you didn't bring a bicycle built for two, otherwise you'd have to pay double duty." Dacre was so taken with the phrase "bicycle built for two" that he decided to use it in a song. That song, "Daisy Bell", first became successful in a London music hall, in a performance by Kate Lawrence.

○ Some history books state that Pierre and Ernest Michaux, the French father-and-son team of carriage-makers, invented the first bicycle during the 1860s. Historians now disagree and there is evidence that the bicycle is older than that. However, historians do agree that Ernest Michaux did invent the modern bicycle pedal and cranks in 1861.

○ Leonardo da Vinci sketched a facsimile of the modern bicycle in 1490. The sketch never progressed beyond the drawing board.

Literacy Links

Oral Language

○ Discuss bicycles. If available, bring one into the classroom. Point out the various parts of the bike, including the handlebar, pedal, spokes, wheels, and seat. Discuss a bicycle that is built for two people to ride. If possible, show children a photo of a bicycle built for two, which is also called a tandem bike.

○ Teach children the American Sign Language sign for *bicycle* (page 120).

Phonological Awareness

○ Sing the song, stopping on the rhyming word in the second line of each couplet. Challenge the children to fill in the rhyme.

Segmentation

○ Clap the syllables in the name *Daisy*. Find a child in the classroom whose name has two syllables. Sing the song substituting the child's name. *How does it sound?*

Curriculum Connections

Discovery

○ Turn a bicycle (or tricycle) upside down on the floor. Encourage the children to examine the parts of the bicycle (or tricycle). Show the children how to use a clothespin to attach a playing card to the spoke of the bike wheel. What happens when you spin the wheel of the bike?

Dramatic Play

○ Provide wedding props, such as rings, fancy dress, flowers, veil, and other related props. Encourage the children to pretend to "get married."

Gross Motor

○ Encourage the children to lie on their backs and pedal their legs as if riding a bicycle.

○ Make two 10' masking tape lines on the floor. Encourage the children to find a partner. Give each child two beanbags. The children race each other down the masking tape lines while holding the beanbags on the top of their hands and pretending they are riding a bicycle. If a child drops a beanbag he or she has to start again at the beginning of the line.

Language

○ Print *Daisy* on two or three 4" x 12" strips of poster board. Laminate the strips and cut the letters in the name apart using a puzzle cut. Encourage the children to work the puzzles.

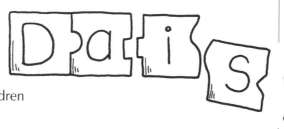

Snack

○ Invite the children to follow the Banana Bicycle Wheels Rebus Recipe (page 99) to make their own snack.

Book Corner

The Bear's Bicycle by Emily Warren McLeod

Bicycle Book by Gail Gibbons

Bicycle Man by Allen Say

Curious George Rides a Bike by H. A. Rey

 English Language Learner Strategy: Using a rebus makes it easier for English language learners to follow the directions.

Writing

❍ Print *Daisy* on chart paper. Encourage the children to copy the name with magnetic letters.

❍ Draw "I ❤ U" on paper. Encourage the children to copy it.

 **Special Needs Adaptation:** The American Sign Language sign for *I Love You* is very easy to learn. It is made with the right hand. Teach the sign to children and encourage them to use the sign with their family and friends. For children who are nonverbal, it can be used to demonstrate affection for family members. The sign is also a good way for children to learn to be kind and affectionate toward each other.

I love you

Home Connection

❍ Encourage children to ask their families to go on a family bike ride.

Airplane Flyers by Pam Schiller

Vocabulary

airplane
dare
flyers
high
lift
nose
race
race
ready
soar
steady
upside down
wave
wings
zoom

Theme Connections

Movement
Spatial Relationships

(Tune: Where, Oh, Where Is Sweet Little Susie?)
Airplane flyers are you ready?
Hold your wings nice and steady.
Start your engines, turn around,
Lift your nose and leave the ground.

Zoom, zoom way up high.
Watch our tricks up in the sky.
We tilt our wing to say hello
To the cheering crowd below.

Soar with me through the air,
Upside down if you dare.
Race the birds or race the bees,
Rest a minute on the breeze.

Zoom, zoom way up high.
Watch our tricks up in the sky.
We tilt our wing to say hello
To the cheering crowd below.

Airplane flyers are you ready?
Hold your wings nice and steady.
Tilt your nose toward the ground,
Slowly land without a sound.

(Before the song starts, ask the children to pretend to put on their goggles and caps and climb into their airplane. Encourage the children to spread their arms to simulate airplane wings and then follow the directions in the lyrics of the song.)

Did You Know?

❍ The Wright Brothers were the first to develop a fully controllable airplane. They understood that flying machines needed to have three-axis control in order for flight to be safe—pitch, roll, and yaw.

❍ To control the pitch of their first glider, they used an elevator mounted in the front of their glider (they called it a "front rudder"). To control roll and to turn, they developed "wing-warping." To control yaw, they perfected the rudder.

❍ Roll is the tilting motion of the airplane when one wing rises or falls in relation to the other. The Wright Brothers used wing warping to control roll, which allowed the edge of one wing to rise up and the edge of the other wing to lower. Today, movable control surfaces called *ailerons* control roll. Roll enables an airplane to bank to the left or right.

❍ Yaw is the twisting motion as the nose turns left or right. Rudders control yaw. Although airplanes use ailerons to turn, rudders are necessary to ensure that the airplane turns more efficiently.

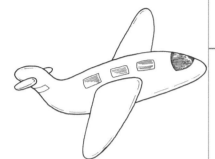

❍ Pitch is the motion of the airplane as its nose points up or down. Today, movable control surfaces called "elevators" are used to control the up and down motion of the airplane along its lateral axis.

❍ See page 19 in "If I Had Wings" for more information about airplanes.

Literacy Links

Comprehension

❍ Teach the children songs, fingerplays, and action rhymes about airplanes (pages 94-96).

Oral Language

❍ Help children make paper airplanes. Encourage the children to fly their planes through the air. Direct them to fly their planes up, down, and upside down. Have them point the noses of their planes up, down, left, and right. Continue giving directions that allow children to practice spatial relationships.

❍ Discuss the importance of keeping airplane wings level. Fill a bucket with blocks. Have a volunteer hold the blocks in one hand and then try to hold her arms out to the side. *Is it difficult to keep both arms parallel with the floor? Why? What would happen if one arm (wing) was lower than the other when the plane was in the sky? When the plane was landing?* Use correct aviation vocabulary when doing this activity. Roll is the tilting motion of the airplane when one wing rises or falls in relation to the other. Movable control surfaces on the wings of an airplane, called ailerons, control roll. Pitch is the term used to refer to the upward and downward direction of the nose of the airplane.

❍ Teach children the American Sign Language sign for *airplane* (page 120).

❍ Share the poem, "Bird's Eye View" with the children.

Bird's Eye View
From way up here I can see
Rooftops, cornfields, and baby deer.
Come fly with me and you will see
The world as viewed by birds and bees.

Curriculum Connections

Blocks

❍ Challenge the children to build an airport complete with runways and towers. Provide airplanes for dramatic play.

○ Build a small town and then take a look at it from above. Have the children discuss what they see.

Construction

○ Help the children make pinwheels. Photocopy the Pinwheel Pattern (page 109) on construction paper. Have the children decorate their pinwheels on both sides. Help the children cut out the pattern. Poke holes where designated. Poke a hole in a straw about 1″ from one end. Fold the pinwheel and secure it with a brad to the straw.

○ Invite the children to make a pair of goggles. Give each child two crates from an egg carton. Help them cut the bottoms out of each crate. Provide pipe cleaners. Show the children how to attach a pipe cleaner to each side of the egg crate to make straps to hold the goggles in place. Provide tempera paint and encourage children to decorate their goggles.

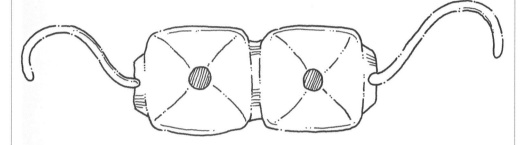

Discovery

○ Place a balance scale in the center. Encourage the children to pretend the balancing trays are airplane wings. Can they balance the wings?

 Special Needs Adaptation: Encourage children with motor challenges to work with partners.

Dramatic Play

○ Provide airplane helmets and goggles for children to explore. Be sure to provide a mirror.

Fine Motor

○ Help the children fold paper airplanes. Encourage them to decorate their paper before folding. Invite the children to fly their airplanes outdoors.

Special Needs Adaptation: Folding and creasing paper for the paper airplanes may require some special assistance. If the child is unable to make his own airplane, try folding the paper with him by placing your hands on his.

Book Corner

Gross Motor

❍ Have the children bend over and look through their legs. *How do things look upside down?* Provide paper and encourage the children to draw what they see.

❍ Lay a 6" strip of masking tape on the floor. Provide a tennis ball. Have the children push the ball with their nose along the strip of tape. Encourage them to keep their "noses off the ground."

❍ Place a ten foot strip of masking tape on the floor. Encourage the children to hold their arms out like airplane wings while walking the line of tape. At the end of the tape have them pretend to take off (jump) like an airplane. Encourage the "airplane flyers" to build speed as they practice their balancing walk.

Outdoors

❍ During outdoor play, on a sunny day, have the children spread their arms like airplane wings and chase their airplane shadows. Ask the children if the shadow they cast looks like an airplane.

❍ See pages 19-21 in "If I Had Wings" for additional airplane activities.

Home Connection

❍ Encourage children to ask family members about their flying experiences.

Little Red Caboose

by Pam Schiller

Vocabulary

back	railroad
behind	red
caboose	smokestack
chug	track
engine	train

Theme Connections

Colors
Sounds

(Tune: Itsy Bitsy Spider)
Little red caboose chug, chug, chug.
Little red caboose chug, chug, chug.
Little red caboose behind the train, train, train.
Smokestack on his back, back, back, back.
Chugging down the track, track, track, track.
Little red caboose behind the train.

Little red caboose chug, chug, chug.
Little red caboose chug, chug, chug.
Little red caboose behind the train, train, train.
Smokestack on his back, back, back, back.
Chugging down the track, track, track, track.
Little red caboose behind the train.

✓ **Special Needs Adaptation:** Children with special needs often have difficulty with social skills, which are essential to making friends and getting along with others. It is often difficult for a child with behavior issues to wait in line or to take a turn. Use this song as an opportunity to discuss that one doesn't have to always be first in line or first at something. When the class is moving from place to place, talk about the importance of being the caboose (or the person at the end of the line). Explain that the caboose is an important position because it keeps the rest of the train safe. Encourage children to volunteer to be the caboose or the last person in line.

Did You Know?

❍ A caboose is a rail transport vehicle at the end of a freight train.

❍ The purpose of the caboose is to allow the train to be supervised from the rear and ensure that cars from the train cannot separate without the crew's knowledge. Should the train break apart in the middle, the crew on the caboose can apply the brakes on the trailing portion and signal for assistance. This allows the locomotive crew to concentrate on events ahead.

❍ The caboose is also used to monitor the cars and the load on the train, making sure there are no problems—load shifting dangerously, overheating axle boxes on the cars (hot boxes) that could cause fire, and so on. A caboose is also fitted with red lights called "markers" to enable the rear of the train to be seen at night. This has led to the phrase "bringing up the markers" to describe the last car on a train.

○ Until the 1980s, laws in the United States and Canada required that all freight trains had a caboose. Today, use of a caboose is rare, making it almost obsolete.

Literacy Links

Comprehension
○ Teach the children fingerplays and action rhymes about trains (pages 95-96).

Letter Knowledge
○ Print the song on chart paper. Have the children help you locate all the "c" letters in the song. Underline each "c". Count how many you find. *Is there a word that begins with a "c" in every line?*

Phonological Awareness
○ Challenge children to find all the words in the song that rhyme with *track*. *What other words rhyme with* track?

Curriculum Connections

Art
○ Provide red paint and encourage the children to paint a red caboose.

Blocks
○ Provide strips of black construction paper for children to use to create a train track. How long a track can they build? Encourage the children to use the blocks to make trains and buildings along the train tracks.

Dramatic Play
○ Paint a large box red and let the children pretend it is a caboose. Add other props, such as a bedroll, conductor's hat, and so on to encourage dramatic play.

Fine Motor
○ Photocopy and enlarge the caboose from the Train Patterns (pages 112-113). Color the caboose, laminate it, and cut it into puzzle pieces. Invite the children to work the Caboose Puzzle.

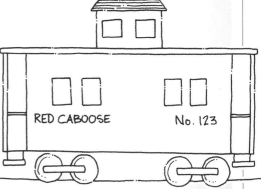

*The Caboose Who
    Got Loose* by Bill
    Peet
*The Little Red
    Caboose* by Steve
    Metzger
*The Little Red
    Caboose* by
    Marian Potter

Gross Motor

○ Make a caboose by painting a shoebox red and add black poster board wheels. Use masking tape to make a throw line. Invite the children to toss a beanbag from the throw line into the caboose. For extra fun, place a service bell inside the caboose and challenge the children to ring the bell.

Math

○ Photocopy the Train Patterns (pages 112-113). Make one engine, one caboose, and six cars. Color the engine, caboose, and cars and laminate them. Make Numeral Cards. Print the numerals 1-6 on index cards. Have the children draw a number from the Numeral Cards and then arrange the train cars accordingly. For example, if the child draws a four, she will lay out one engine, four cars, and one caboose. If the child draws a six, she will lay out one engine, six cars, and one caboose.

Snack

○ Encourage the children to use graham crackers, cream cheese, and round pretzels to make cabooses.

Writing

○ Trace magnetic letters to form *caboose* on sheets of drawing paper. Leave blank space for the "o"s. Provide magnetic letters and encourage the children to lay the letters over your letters to fill in the missing letters.

Home Connection

○ Encourage children to ask their families to watch a train crossing an intersection. Suggest they count the cars and have them report back as to whether or not the train had a caboose.

Windshield Wiper

(Tune: Row, Row, Row Your Boat)
I'm a little windshield wiper,
Back and forth I go.
Swish, swish, swish, swash,
Oh, how the rain does flow!

I'm a little windshield wiper,
Back and forth I go.
No matter how hard it rains,
I'll keep your windshield clean.

Vocabulary

back and forth
clean
rain
swash
swish
windshield
windshield wiper

Theme Connections

Sounds
Weather

Did You Know?

❍ There are three components to a windshield wiper: the arm, the blade, and the wiping element.
❍ Good windshield wiper function is important for car safety. Worn windshield wipers can seriously compromise driver vision when road conditions are wet or icy.
❍ Windshield wiper blades need to be replaced every six months.

Literacy Links

Letter Knowledge/Phonological Awareness

❍ Print *windshield wiper* on chart paper. Ask children to identify the first letter in each word. Have the children say "windshield wiper." Point out the repetitive sound of the initial consonant in each word. Point out that this is called *alliteration*.

Oral Language

❍ Discuss the use of windshield wipers. *When do we use them?*
❍ Print *windshield* on chart paper. Draw a line between *wind* and *shield*. Point out that windshield is made up of two words *wind* and *shield*. Explain that this makes windshield a *compound word*.

✓ **Special Needs Adaptation:** Provide more practice with compound words. Explain that a compound word is two words that fit together. Make a list of other compound words, such as *cupcake, outside, inside,* and *baseball,* to reinforce what you are teaching.

Phonological Awareness

❍ Discuss the *onomatopoeic* words (words that imitate the sounds they are describing) in the song. In the song, *swish, swash* is used to describe the sound of washer wiping. *What other sounds might be described using* swish, swash?

Curriculum Connections

Art

❍ Provide fingerpaint directly on the surface of a table. Provide squeegees and encourage the children to move them through the paint to create designs.

Discovery

❍ Display several pairs of windshield wipers. Auto repair shops will happily give you worn out wipers. Encourage the children to find the arm, the blade, and the wiping element.

Dramatic Play

❍ Provide paper towels and water in a spray bottle. Encourage the children to clean the windows in the classroom.

Field Trip

❍ Take a walk to a parking lot. Look at windshield wipers on different vehicles. *Are they all alike? Are they all the same size?*

Gross Motor

❍ Tape bulletin board paper on a wall. Give the children crayons. Encourage them to hold a crayon in each hand and move their arms back and forth like windshield wipers. Have the children stand back and look at the resulting design. *Is the design different if you move the "wipers" (arms) in the same direction as it is when you move the "wipers" in opposite directions?*

Movement

❍ Have the children lie on their backs on the floor. Tell them that the floor is the window and their legs are the wipers. Encourage them to use their legs

Listen to the Rain by Bill Martin, Jr.
Rain by Robert Kalan
Rain Drop Splash by Alvin Tresselt
The Wheels on the Bus by Paul O. Zelinsky

as wipers by moving them open and shut. Challenge them to use their arms as wipers. Can they work with a friend to use other body parts as wipers?

Music
❍ Sing "The Wheels on the Bus" (page 78) with the children. Make sure to emphasize the verse about wipers (*The wipers on the bus go swish, swish, swish…*).

Sand and Water Play
❍ Make Sand Combs by cutting a pattern in one edge of a 4" x 12" strip of poster board or card stock. Provide a tray of sand and Sand Combs. Invite children to use the combs to move the sand. Discuss how the blade of the Sand Comb is similar to the blade of a windshield wiper.

Home Connection

❍ Encourage the children to show their families the parts of a windshield wiper on the family car.

My Bonnie Lies Over the Ocean

Vocabulary

blow
Bonnie
bring back
ocean
sea
wind

Theme Connections

Friends and Families
Oceans
Weather

My Bonnie lies over the ocean.
My Bonnie lies over the sea.
My Bonnie lies over the ocean.
Oh, bring back my Bonnie to me.

Chorus:
Bring back, bring back,
Oh, bring back my Bonnie to me,
   to me.
Bring back, bring back,
Oh, bring back my Bonnie to me.

Oh blow ye the winds o'er the
   ocean,
And blow ye the winds o'er the
   sea.
Oh blow ye the winds o'er the
   ocean,
And bring back my Bonnie to me.

(Chorus)

The winds have blown over the
   ocean.
The winds have blown over the
   sea.
The winds have blown over the
   ocean,
And brought back my bonnie to
   me.

Did You Know?

❍ "My Bonnie Lies Over the Ocean" is a traditional Scottish folksong.
❍ Some people believe that the song refers to Bonnie Prince Charles.
❍ This song is a popular camp song.
❍ The Beatles recorded a variation of this song in 1961 in Germany. They recorded an English version and a German version of the song.

Literacy Links

Listening
❍ Encourage the children to stand or sit each time they sing (or hear) *Bonnie*.

✔ **Special Needs Adaptation:** If a child cannot stand, ask him to raise his arm each time he hears *Bonnie* in the song. Or he can hold up a sign or ring a small service bell each time *Bonnie* is sung.

Phonological Awareness
❍ Clap the syllables in *Bonnie*. Change Bonnie to another two-syllable name and sing the song again.

Print Awareness
❍ Invite the children to brainstorm a list of ways that someone might travel across the ocean.

Curriculum Connections

Art
❍ Provide blue and green tempera paint. Encourage the children to paint an ocean.
❍ Provide blue and green fingerpaint. Provide combs and encourage children to drag them through the paint to create designs in the "ocean." As an alternative, use shaving cream colored with green and blue food coloring as fingerpaint.

Construction
❍ Cut out the inner circles of paper plates. Give two paper plate rims to each child. Help them tape blue cellophane or clear plastic to the inside of each plate. Invite them to glue fish, shells, sand, and seaweed to the cellophane (on the inside of the plates) and then glue the paper plates together to make an ocean scene.

Discovery
❍ Provide items that create a wind, such as a hand fan, a squeeze bottle, or a paper plate. Invite the children to use these "wind makers" to move a feather across a table.

Math
❍ Provide a variety of shells for the children to sort and classify.

Science

- Provide photos of animals. Encourage the children to sort the photos by those that live in the ocean and those who do not.

- Make Ocean Bottles. Fill a liter bottle half full with water. Put two to three drops of blue and green food coloring into the bottle and shake. Fill remainder of the bottle with cooking oil. Glue the top on the bottle using hot glue (adult-only step). Do not shake. Encourage the children to hold the bottle horizontally until clear, then raise and lower each end to create waves.

Snack

- Invite the children to help make blue gelatin. Add gummy fish to complete the ocean effect. Serve it as an Ocean Delight.

Home Connection

- Encourage children to ask their family members if they know this song and to sing the song with their family members.

Book Corner

Can You See the Wind? by Allan Fowler

Oceans by Seymour Simon

Over in the Ocean: In a Coral Reef by Marianne Berkes

The Wind Blew by Pat Hutchins

The Wheels on the Bus

The wheels on the bus go round
  and round,
Round and round, round and
  round.
The wheels on the bus go round
  and round,
All through the town.

The wipers on the bus go swish,
  swish, swish,
Swish, swish, swish, swish, swish,
  swish.
The wipers on the bus go swish,
  swish, swish,
All through the town.

The horn on the bus goes beep,
  beep, beep,
Beep, beep, beep, beep, beep,
  beep.
The horn on the bus goes beep,
  beep, beep,
All through the town.

The money on the bus goes clink,
  clink, clink,
Clink, clink, clink, clink, clink,
  clink.
The money on the bus goes clink,
  clink, clink,
All through the town.

The driver on the bus says,
  "Move on back,
Move on back, move on back."
The driver on the bus says,
  "Move on back,"
All through the town.

The baby on the bus says, "Wah,
  wah, wah,
Wah, wah, wah, wah, wah, wah."
The baby on the bus says, "Wah,
  wah, wah,"
All through the town.

The mommy on the bus says,
  "Shush, shush, shush,
Shush, shush, shush, shush,
  shush, shush."
The mommy on the bus says,
  "Shush, shush, shush,"
All through the town.

The wheels on the bus go round
  and round,
Round and round, round and
  round.
The wheels on the bus go round
  and round,
All through the town.

Vocabulary

baby
back
beep
bus
clink
driver
horn
mommy
money
round
shush
swish
town
wheels
windshield wipers

Theme Connections

Community Workers
Movement
Sounds

Did You Know?

○ The word "bus" is a shortened version of omnibus, meaning "a bus for everyone."

○ School buses are the largest mass transit program in the United States. School buses provide approximately 8.8 billion student trips each year. In contrast, city transit buses provide only about 5.2 billion passenger trips each year.

○ Every school day, some 440,000 yellow school buses transport more than 24 million children to and from schools and school-related activities. There is no safer way to transport a child than in a school bus.

Literacy Links

Oral Language

○ Discuss different types of buses. *For what purpose are buses used? What sizes do buses come in?*

○ Discuss the differences between a bus and a car.

Phonological Awareness

○ Discuss the *onomatopoeic* words (words that imitate the sound they are describing) in the song.

Print Awareness

○ Show the children what a bus stop sign looks like. Discuss the use of signs.

○ Help the children make a list of all the things on a bus, for example, wheels, wipers, lights, people, money or tokens, and so on.

> **Special Needs Adaptation:** Extend this activity for children with special needs by working on bus-related vocabulary. Use blank cards and, on each one, write a bus-related word, such as wheels, wipers, lights, and so on. Above each word glue a picture to match it. Invite children to help you make up sentences with each picture as you hold it up. Children with special needs will learn new words more easily if they can relate the new words to an experience. Take the class on a field trip on a bus. If you have a bus or van at the school invite the bus or van driver to give the children a tour of the bus. Invite the children to sit behind the wheel, turn on the wipers, and practice being passengers. Use this song as an opportunity to reinforce bus safety rules.

Curriculum Connections

Art

○ Provide yellow paint and encourage the children to paint a yellow school bus.

Blocks

○ Invite the children to build a town. Encourage them to roll a toy bus through the town.

Discovery

○ Give the children a basket of items to sort into categories of things that roll and things that don't roll. Be sure to include things that will roll without wheels. Discuss what makes something roll.

Dramatic Play

○ Place chairs in sets of two and rows of four to create a bus. Place one chair in the front for the driver. Add props such as a driver's cap, a box for tokens or tickets, a paper plate for a steering wheel, and a squeak toy for a horn. Encourage the children to sing songs while they ride the bus. Demonstrate calling out the names of streets when the bus makes its stops.

Field Trip

○ Take a trip on a city bus.

Games

○ Provide a shallow dish. Create a throw line on the floor with a strip of masking tape. Challenge children to toss bus tokens into the dish. If no bus tokens are available, use coins or bingo markers. *What sound does the token make when it hits the dish?*

Listening

○ Provide items that will make a swishing sound such as squeeze bottles, fans, and basters. Invite the children to explore making a swishing sound. Provide a pie tin and items to make a clinking sound such as coins, washers, and buttons. Invite the children to explore clinking sounds.

Math

○ Provide a vehicle with big wheels and one with smaller wheels. Place a small piece of masking tape for a marker on the rim of one of the wheels on each vehicle. Prepare a start line by placing a strip of masking tape on the floor. Line both vehicles up on the start line with the masking tape marker lined up with the line on the floor. Have the children push each vehicle until the tape moves around one time. Mark each ending point on the floor. *Which vehicle moves the greatest distance with just one rotation of the wheel?*

○ Provide jars with numerals one through five printed or taped on the side. Provide 15 tokens or coins. Have the children place the number of tokens in each container that corresponds with the numeral on the side.

○ See pages 72-74 in "Windshield Wipers" for additional activities.

Home Connection

○ Encourage families to take their children on a bus ride.

The Train by Richele Bartkowiak

(Tune: Row, Row, Row Your Boat)
Ride, ride, ride the train.
Where would you like to go?
Clickety, clickety, clickety, clack,
Just let the conductor know.

Ride, ride, ride the train
To cities near and far.
Sit back, relax, enjoy the ride
In the passenger car.

Ride, ride, ride the train
So many places to see.
Like Arizona and Idaho,
New York and Tennessee.

Ride, ride, ride the train
Our journey's at an end.
Clickety, clickety, clickety, clack,
Can't wait to ride again!

Vocabulary

Arizona
clack
clickety
conductor
far
Idaho
journey
near
New York
passenger car
ride
Tennessee

Theme Connections

Community Workers
Sounds
Travel

Did You Know?

○ Trains became a means of travel in America in 1825. At that time, some people were frightened of traveling by train. They thought trains moving at a speed of more than 12 miles per hour would make them suffer from mental problems. They also feared that they could have the air sucked right out of their lungs by traveling at such a dangerous speed.

○ The first transcontinental railway (a railroad that passes from one end of a continent to the other) in the United States was completed in 1869.

○ Train travel is the most popular form of transport in Europe.

Literacy Links

Comprehension

○ Teach the children fingerplays and action rhymes about trains (pages 95-96).

Oral Language

○ Discuss the similarities and differences between trains and buses.

○ Teach children the American Sign Language sign for *train*.

Phonological Awareness

○ Point out the *alliteration* (repetition of a beginning consonant) in the song, for example, "clickety, clack."

Print Awareness

○ Have the children dictate a story about where the train is going. Write it down for them to "read."

○ Show the children where Idaho, Tennessee, Arizona, and New York are on a globe or a map. Point to the name or initials of each state. Discuss the shape of each state. Show the children their state. Show them railroad markings on a map.

train

Curriculum Connections

Art

○ Encourage children to draw a picture of a place they would like to travel to by train or simply to draw a picture of a train. Invite them to dictate a sentence about their drawing.

○ Cut sponges into train shapes. Provide tempera paint and encourage the children to make train prints.

Fine Motor

○ Photocopy the engine from the Train Patterns (pages 112-113). Color it, cut it out, laminate it, and glue a magnetic strip or large paper clip to the back. Draw train tracks on a sheet of poster board. Be sure to make a starting location and an ending spot. Place the train on the tracks and encourage the children to move the train by using a large magnet under the poster board to guide the train down the track.

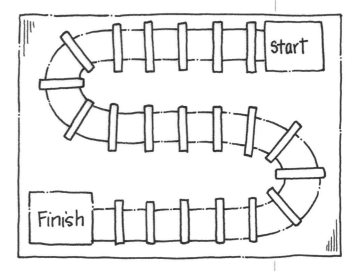

Book Corner

Chugga Chugga Choo Choo by Kevin Lewis

Terrific Trains by Tony Mitton

Train Song by Diane Siebert

Trains by Gallimard Jeunesse

Language

❍ Photocopy the Train Patterns (pages 112-113). Color the copies, cut them out, glue photos of circus animals inside the cars, laminate them, and glue them to craft sticks. Encourage the children to use the train puppets to retell the story of "Engine Ninety Nine" (page 97).

❍ Make photocopies of the Train Rhyming Word Cards (pages 116-118). Color the cards, cut them out, and laminate them. Invite the children to sort the cards into the things that rhyme with *train* and those that do not.

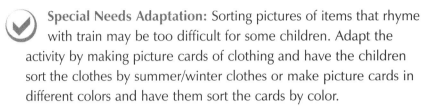 **Special Needs Adaptation:** Sorting pictures of items that rhyme with train may be too difficult for some children. Adapt the activity by making picture cards of clothing and have the children sort the clothes by summer/winter clothes or make picture cards in different colors and have them sort the cards by color.

Listening/Story Time

❍ Read the listening story, "Engine Ninety-Nine" (page 97). After you have read the story, ask children questions about the story. *What color was Engine Ninety-Nine? What job would you like if you were a train engine? Do you think Engine Ninety-Nine would like to haul children? Why?*

Math

❍ Photocopy the Train Patterns (pages 112-113). Color them, cut them out, and laminate them. Invite the children to put the train together with the engine, followed by four cars, and then the caboose. Provide a measuring tape. Have the children measure the length of the train. Remove a car and measure again. *What happens to the length of the train?*

Snack

❍ Serve round ice cream sandwiches as train wheels.

❍ See pages 31-33 in "Clickety Clack," pages 59-61 in "This Little Train," pages 25-27 in "Down by the Station," and pages 70-71 in "Little Red Caboose" for additional train activities.

Home Connection

❍ Encourage the children to look through magazines or newpapers with their families and locate someplace they would like to travel to by train. Ask the children to bring pictures of their travel choices to school for discussion.

Dip, Dip, and Swing

Vocabulary

bright
dip
flashing
flight
keen
paddles
silver
swing
wild goose

Theme Connections

Movement
Sounds

My paddles keen and bright,
Flashing with silver
Follow the wild goose flight.
Dip, dip, and swing.
Dip, dip, and swing.
(Repeat)

Did You Know?

○ For many people, paddling a canoe provides a quiet, stress-free calm that comes with heading out alone and under one's own power. Other people enjoy the cooperative effort of paddling with a partner. Paddling in tandem is not as easy as it may sound.

○ Canoes are the most common type of boat used by Native Americans. Long and narrow, with gently rounded bottoms and no keel, they taper toward the bow and stern. They are generally propelled by using paddles or poles.

○ North American Indians made two basic types of canoes. In the eastern woodlands and along the Pacific Coast, they crafted dugouts made from large logs that had been hollowed out. In the sub-Arctic and Arctic, as well as on the plateau and in the northern portions of the eastern woodlands, native people built wooden frames for their canoes and covered them with bark or animal hides. Eastern Indians generally covered their canoes with birch or elm bark. In the West and in the Arctic, canoe builders used animal hides, such as caribou, moose, and walrus, to cover the frames. Both types of canoes ranged in size from small boats 8 to 10 feet long, designed to carry 1 to 3 people, to much larger boats capable of carrying more than 40 people.

○ See page 43 for more information on canoes.

canoe

Literacy Links

Oral Language

❍ Discuss the words in the song that may be new vocabulary like *flashing*, *keen*, *bright*, *silver*, *wild goose*, *dip*, and *swing*. Discuss paddling to the rhythm of the song and paddling with another person.

❍ Display photos of Native American canoes. Discuss the techniques Indians used to make canoes.

❍ Teach the children the American Sign Language sign for *canoe*.

Print Awareness

❍ Print the song on chart paper. Move your hand under the words as you sing the song. Point out the left-to-right and top-to-bottom movement of the print.

Curriculum Connections

Art

❍ Tape a sheet of butcher paper to the wall. Provide blue tempera paint. Have the children paint a design by dipping their brush in the paint and then swinging it across the paper. Provide a rhythm or cadence (dip, swing, dip, swing, dip, and so on) and encourage the children to chant the rhythm while they paint.

Discovery

❍ Provide a few pieces of silverware and a silver-polishing cloth. **Note**: Be sure to use a silver-polishing cloth and not silver polish, which can be harmful to children. Invite the children to polish the silver. Talk with them as they work. *Is the silver shiny when it is tarnished? Is it shiny after it is polished?* Shine a light on the silver. *What happens?* Take a silver item outdoors in the sun. *What happens when the sun hits the silver?*

Dramatic Play

❍ Provide a large box to use as a canoe. Invite the children to sit in the box, two at a time, and pretend to paddle in tandem. Have the child in the front set the rhythm by saying "dip, swing, dip, swing, dip…".

Fine Motor/Snack

❍ Give the children a metal spoon and half of mellon. Show them how to use the spoon to scrape out the flesh of the melon. Point out that American Indians made canoes by scraping out the center of a tree trunk. Let the children eat the melon for snack.

Math

○ Provide a variety of small boxes to represent canoes. Give the children empty thread spools to represent people. Suggest that the children figure out how many people fit into each canoe.

> **Special Needs Adaptation:** Make this a cooperative activity. Ask one child to be a peer buddy and help the child with special needs count the number of "spool people" in each canoe. Ask the children to take turns counting the people in each canoe. Use phrases including "more people" or "fewer people" when talking to the child about the people in the canoe.

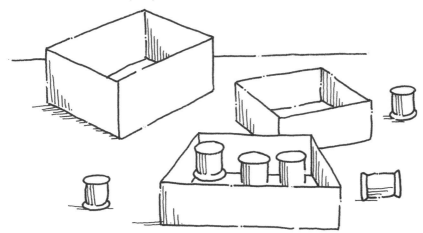

Outdoors

○ Encourage the children to try some tandem exercises. Ask children to select a partner. Have them: sit down, place their feet together, and pedal in tandem; turn a rope in tandem; stand side by side and walk with their inside legs touching; as well as any other exercises that require working together with a partner.

Water Play

○ Provide toy canoes and other boats to float in a tub of water.

Writing

○ Print *dip* and *swing* on index cards. Provide magnetic letters and encourage the children to use the letters to copy the words.

Home Connection

○ Encourage children to ask their family members if they have ever paddled a canoe. Encourage the children to get the details.

A Canoe Trip by Bobbie Kalman

Canoe Days by Gary Paulsen

Row, Row, Row Your Boat by Heather Collins

Three Days on a River in a Red Canoe by Vera B. Williams

SONGS AND ACTIVITIES

City Travel additional verses by
Pam Schiller and Richele Bartkowiak

(Tune: Pop! Goes the Weasel)
I drive the bus around the town.
I'll meet you at the corner.
Just drop your token in the slot.
"Swish" goes the door.

A dollar for a ride across town
Or to the park and ride.
Find a seat and hold on tight.
"Swish" goes the door.

I drive a taxi around the town.
Yellow fenders clean and bright
I stop for all the folks who wave.
"Beep, beep," goes the horn.

I'll drive you down the road a bit.
I'll take you round the corner.
The meter starts when you close
the door.
"Beep, beep," goes the horn.

Vocabulary

beep	seat
bit	slot
bright	swish
bus	taxi
clean	tight
corner	token
dollar	town
fender	wave
horn	yellow
meter	

Theme Connections

Community Workers
Sounds

Did You Know?

❍ A taxicab is a popular form of public transportation.
❍ Gottlieb Daimler built the world's first taxi in 1897. It was called the Daimler Victoria and had a taxi meter. That same year, the taxi was delivered to Stuttgart, Germany transportation entrepreneur Friedrich Greiner. He used it to start the world's first motorized taxi company.
❍ There are 40,000 licensed taxi drivers and 11,787 licensed taxicabs in New York City. New York City cab drivers average about 30 fares a day.
❍ See page 79 for information about buses.

Literacy Links

Oral Language
❍ Encourage the children to describe the similarities and differences between buses and taxis.
❍ Teach the children the American Sign Language signs for *taxi* (page 121) and *bus* (page 120).

Phonological Awareness
❍ Discuss the *onomatopoeic* words in the song, *swish* and *beep*. Explain that onomatopoeic words are words that imitate the sound they are describing.

What other onomatopoeic word might be used to describe the sound of the horn? (honk)

○ Teach children the poem "Maxi's Taxi."

Maxi's Taxi
Maxi drives a taxi with a beep, beep, beep,
He picks up all the people in a heap, heap, heap,
Through the traffic he creeps, creeps, creeps,
And when his day is over he sleeps, sleeps, sleeps.

Print Awareness/Letter knowledge

○ Make a "Bus Stop" sign. Provide crayons and encourage the children to copy it to make their own signs.

Curriculum Connections

Blocks

○ Invite children to build a town. Fold small pieces of tagboard into tents and print *taxi* on top of them. Tape them to the top of vehicles. Encourage the children to run taxis through the town.

Discovery

○ Give the children a dollar bill and a magnifying glass to explore it. Challenge children to find specific things such as the numeral 1, an eye in a strange place, a pyramid, and specific letters, for example, u, s, t, d.

Field Trip

○ Take the children on a bus ride. Point out the token box or ticket taker, the windshield wipers, doors that open and close, horn, and so on.

Listening/Math

○ Provide a squeak horn or a squeak toy to represent a horn. Ask children to create a honking pattern. For example, two quick honks and a pause before a third honk, and then repeat the pattern.

Movement

○ Teach the children how to spell *taxi* with their bodies. For the "t" suggest they stand with their arms out to the side. For the "a", have them put their hands together over their head. For the "x" suggest they cross their arms

Book Corner

The Adventures of Taxi Dog by Debra Sal Barracca

Big Yellow Taxi by Ken Wilson-Max

Don't Let the Pigeon Drive the Bus by Mo Willems

over their head and for the "I" put their arms together as straight as possible over their head. Challenge children to think of ways they can make the first letter of their name. Make sure they know it is okay if they want to ask a friend to help them make their letter.

Music and Movement
❍ Give the children pompoms to make a swishing sound while they dance to instrumental music. If pompoms are not available, make some. Arrange a small handful of crimped basket stuffing such as Easter egg grass so it all faces in the same direction. Use a small piece of vinyl tape to wrap a bunch together and create a handle for the pompom. Trim close to the tape.

Outdoors
❍ Set up a bus stop and encourage the children to pretend their tricycles are buses, or encourage the children to use their tricycles as taxis. Suggest they pick up passengers and deliver them to spots on the playground. Because some children in the class may not have ridden in a taxi, locate pictures of taxis and taxi drivers. Talk about what a taxi is for and what it does, and how it is different from a family car. Repeat the activity with a bus. Many children may ride the bus to school, but might be unaware that buses are also a form of public transportation.

> **Special Needs Adaptation:** Certain children with special needs will depend on public transportation when they get older, so it is important that they know the vocabulary associated with public transportation.

Writing
❍ Print *taxi* several times in large print on a sheet of butcher paper. Provide tempera paint and small cars. Encourage the children to drive the cars through the paint and then move the cars over the letters in "taxi."

Home Connection

❍ Suggest that families take their children on bus rides or on short taxi rides.

Put Your Little Foot

Vocabulary

foot
here
little
put
there
turn
walk

Theme Connections

Movement
Parts of the Body

Chorus:
Put your little foot,
Put your little foot,
Put your little foot right there.
Put your little foot,
Put your little foot,
Put your little foot right there.

Walk and walk, walk
And turn.
Walk and walk, walk
And turn.
Walk and walk, walk
And turn.
Walk and walk, walk
And turn.

(Chorus)

Hop and hop, hop
And turn.
Hop and hop, hop
And turn.
Hop and hop, hop
And turn.
Hop and hop, hop
And turn.

(Chorus)

Skip and skip, skip
And turn.
Skip and skip, skip
And turn.
Skip and skip, skip
And turn.
Skip and skip, skip
And turn.

(Chorus)

Did You Know?

❍ Our feet have 52 bones in them, one quarter of all the bones in the body.
❍ Each foot is able to absorb pressure of more than one ton per square inch. Bones and ligaments of the feet spread this force and send it efficiently through the leg bones.
❍ There are about 250,000 sweat glands in a pair of feet, and they excrete up to a half-pint of moisture each day.
❍ Experts recommend taking 10,000 steps a day for health. A pedometer measures the number of steps we take.
❍ The record for the person with the biggest feet in the world is held by an American, Robert Wadlow. His feet were 18 ½ inches (47cm) long and he wore size 37 shoes! He was nearly nine feet tall when he died in 1940.
❍ President Abraham Lincoln wore a size 14 shoe.
❍ See page 40 in "Walk, Walk, Walk Your Feet" for more information about feet and walking.

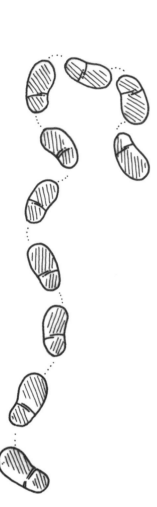

Literacy Links

Letter Knowledge

❍ Place magnetic letters randomly on the floor. Have the children sing along with the song putting their foot on a letter in their name each time the song says "right there."

❍ Print *foot* and *feet* on chart paper. Read each word. Ask the children which letters are alike in each word. *Which letters are different? What letter is the first letter in each word? What letter is the last letter in each word?*

Oral Language

❍ Teach the children the American Sign Language sign for *foot* (page 121). Encourage the children to use the sign for *foot* when they sing the song.

Curriculum Connections

Discovery

❍ Have the children take off their shoes and examine each other's feet with a magnifying glass. Discuss the parts of the feet with children as they are looking at a friend's feet. *Where are the toenails? Which toe is the big toe? What is the small toe called? Do everyone's feet look alike?*

Dramatic Play

❍ Fill the center with different types of shoes and other foot-related items, such as skates and skis. Discuss the many types of shoes. *Which shoes are soft? Which shoes are hard? Which shoes are good for running and playing? Which shoes are worn when we dress up?*

Games

❍ Play Twister. If you do not have a commercial game, make your own game. Paint hands and feet on a shower curtain liner. Make a die for the game by taping down the top of a pint milk carton and covering it with white paper. Draw colored hands and feet on the sides of the die.

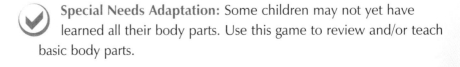 **Special Needs Adaptation:** Some children may not yet have learned all their body parts. Use this game to review and/or teach basic body parts.

Gross Motor

○ Place a service bell on the floor. Invite the children to take off their shoes and tap the bell with their feet, first with their eyes open and then with their eyes closed.

○ Place a line of masking tape on the floor. Ask children to walk the line in a pattern of "walk, walk, walk, turn; walk, walk, walk, turn." After children are able to do the pattern walk, challenge them to try it with a beanbag on their head.

○ Encourage children to select a partner for a Three Leg Race. Have partners stand side by side. Use wide ribbon to tie their inside legs together. Create a start and a finish line with masking tape. Have two sets of partners race each other. *Why is it difficult to walk this way? What makes it easier?*

Language

○ Photocopy the patterns of the Finger Puppets (page 106). Cut out the puppets. Invite the children to color the puppets and then put them on their fingers and "walk" them around. Suggest they try putting the puppet feet "here" and "there."

Writing

○ Provide index cards with *foot* and *feet* printed on them. Encourage the children to "walk" their fingers over the letters. Provide tracing paper and crayons so the children can trace the words.

Home Connection

○ Suggest that families compare shoe sizes. *Who has the largest foot? Who has the smallest foot?*

Baby Dance by Ann Taylor
The Hokey Pokey by Sheila Hamanaka
The Listening Walk by Paul Showers

More Learning and Fun

Songs

All Though the Sky

(Tune: The Wheels on the Bus)
The pilot on the plane says, "Fasten your belts,
   (*fasten seat belts*)
Fasten your belts, fasten your belts."
The pilot on the airplane says, "Fasten your belts
The pilot on the airplane says, "Fasten your belts
Before we start to fly."

The seats on the plane go back and forth, (*move
   back and forth*)
Back and forth, back and forth.
The seats on the plane go back and forth
All through the sky.

Additional verses:
The lights on the plane go blink, blink, blink…
   (*fingers and thumbs together and then apart*)
The attendants on the plane say tea or soda…
   (*hold out left and then right hand*)

Did You Ever See an Airplane?

(Tune: Did You Ever See a Lassie?)
Did you ever see an airplane,
An airplane, an airplane?
Did you ever see an airplane
Way up in the sky?

Big ones and small ones
And short ones and tall ones.
Did you ever see an airplane
Way up in the sky?

Flying

(Tune: Row, Row, Row Your Boat)
Fly, fly, fly the plane.
Way up in the sky.
Trees and houses,
Cars and people,
Zooming, zooming by.

I'm a Train

(Tune: I'm a Texas Star)
I'm a train, I'm a train,
I'm a traveling train.
I ride in the sun and I ride in the rain.
My wheels roll down the railroad track
Singing a song of clackety clack.
Chugga chugga, chug, chug
Choo! Choo!

I've Been Working on the Railroad

I've been working on the railroad,
All the livelong day.
I've been working on the railroad,
Just to pass the time away.

Can't you hear the whistle blowing?
Rise up so early in the morn.
Can't you hear the captain shouting,
Dinah, blow your horn?

Dinah, won't you blow,
Dinah, won't you blow,
Dinah, won't you blow your horn?
Dinah, won't you blow,
Dinah, won't you blow,
Dinah, won't you blow your horn?
Someone's in the kitchen with Dinah.
Someone's in the kitchen, I know.

Someone's in the kitchen with Dinah.
Strumming on the old banjo,
And singing,
"Fee, fi, fiddle-e-i-o.
Fee, fi, fiddle-e-i-o-o-o-o.
Fee, fi, fiddle-e-i-o."
Strumming on the old banjo.

The Plane Is in the Sky

(Tune: The Farmer in the Dell)
The plane is in the sky,
The plane is in the sky,
Zooming through the air we go,
The plane is in the sky.

The pilot's in control,
The pilot's in control,
Zooming through the air we go,
The pilot's in control.

The clouds are sailing by,
The clouds are sailing by,
Zooming through the air we go,
The clouds are sailing by.

The plane is floating down,
The plane is floating down,
Softly to the ground we go,
The plane is floating down.

Fingerplays and Action Rhymes

The Airplane

The airplane has great big wings (*stretch out arms*)
Its propeller spins 'round and sings,
Vvvvvvrrruuuummmmm. (*move arms around in a circle.*)
The airplane goes up. (*lift up arms*)
The airplane dips down.
The airplane flies—'round all of the town! (*fly around—arms outstretched*)

As It Goes

As it goes,
Little red train
Just grows and grows.
(*One child "chugs" around the room as the train, or have two trains and two children "chug" around the room, each representing a train. At the end of the verse the first child invites a second child to hook on to his or her train. Repeat until all children are part of the train or until the children tire of the game.*)

Choo Choo Train

This is a choo choo train (*bend elbows*)
Puffing down the track, (*rotate arms in rhythm*)
Now it's going forward, (*push forward, continue rotating motion*)
Now it's going back. (*pull arms back, continue rotating motion*)
Now the bell is ringing, (*pretend to pull the cord— ding ding*)
Now the whistle blows. (*hold fist near mouth and toot toot*)
What a lot of noise it makes (*cover ears*)
Everywhere it goes. (*stretch out arms*)

Crocodile

If you should meet a crocodile
Don't take a stick and poke him;
Ignore the welcome of his smile,
Be careful not to stroke him.
For as he sleeps upon the Nile
He gets thinner and thinner
And whene'er you meet a crocodile,
He's looking for his dinner.

Here Comes the Choo Choo Train

Here comes the choo choo train
Coming down the track.
First it's going forward,
Then it's going back.
Hear the bells ringing, ding a ling, ding a ling,
Hear the whistle blowing, woo woo,
What a lot of noise it makes
Everywhere it goes!

I Have a Little Wagon

I have a little wagon *(hold hand out palm up)*
It goes everywhere with me. *(move had around)*
I can pull it, *(pull hand toward you)*
I can push it. *(push hand away from you)*
I can turn it upside down. *(turn hand upside down)*

Motor Boat

Motor boat, motor boat,
Go so fast.
Motor boat, motor boat.
Step on the gas.

Motor boat, motor boat,
Go so fast.
Motor boat, motor boat,
Make a big splash.

My Airplane

If I had an airplane, *(use hand as an airplane)*
Zoom, zoom, zoom,
I'd fly to Mexico. *(fly hand through the air)*
Wave my hand and off I'd go. *(wave)*
If I had an airplane, *(use hand as an airplane)*
Zoom, zoom, zoom.

My Bike

One wheel, two wheels *(make circles with thumb and index finger for wheels)*
On the ground,
My feet make the pedals *(lift feet and pretend to pedal bike)*
Go round and round.
The handlebars help me *(pretend to steer)*
Steer so straight,
Down the sidewalk *(shade eyes as if looking at something in the distance)*
And through the gate.

Three Little Monkeys

Three little monkeys
Swinging in a tree
Teasing Mr. Crocodile,
"You can't catch me."
Along comes Mr. Crocodile,
Quiet as can be
And he SNAPS that monkey
Right out of the tree.
SNAP!

Two little monkeys
Swinging in a tree
Teasing Mr. Crocodile,
"You can't catch me."
Along comes Mr. Crocodile,
Quiet as can be
And he SNAPS that monkey
Right out of the tree.
SNAP!

One little monkey
Swinging in a tree
Teasing Mr. Crocodile,
"You can't catch me."
Along comes Mr. Crocodile,
Quiet as can be
And he SNAPS that monkey
Right out of the tree.
SNAP!

No more little monkeys sitting in a tree!

Stories

My Little Red Wagon
(Flannel Board Story)

Directions: Trace the patterns (see pages 107-108) onto Pelon. Color them and cut them out.

One day my Aunt Richele came to play with me. We took my red wagon and we started down the sidewalk. At the end of the block we saw Mrs. Markle working in her yard. She gave us a pretty plant. We put it in the wagon.

When we rolled past the empty lot, I saw something in the grass. A rock! We put it in the wagon.

Around the corner, the Bartkowiak's were having a yard sale. Aunt Richele bought a birdcage. We put it in the wagon. I bought a toy car. We put it in the wagon.

The wagon was getting crowded with the rock and the plant and the toy car and the birdcage, so we headed home. Just as we started up the driveway, my dog Comet came from out of nowhere and jumped in the wagon! What do you think happened?

The wagon tipped over and everything spilled out—the rock, the plant, the toy car, the birdcage, and Comet! What a mess! We picked up everything. Then Richele put ME in the wagon and took me home.

Engine Ninety-Nine by Pam Schiller (Listening Story)

Even before the first coat of the shiny black paint on his smokestack was dry, little Engine 99 knew what kind of a train he wanted to be. He didn't want to pull tank cars full of chemicals. He didn't want to pull cars full of passengers. He didn't want to pull heavy equipment. He wanted to be a circus train. He wanted to pull cars full of elephants, giraffes, bears, and lions. He loved animals. He had been dreaming of being a circus train ever since the mechanics tightened the first bolts on his wheels.

Now it was his moment. Soon someone would start his engine, and he would begin to work just like the other trains in the station. He was so excited he wanted to toot his horn, but he stood quiet and still, hoping that someone would declare him ready for work.

He stood still all day and all night and all day again. Would anyone ever come for him? He saw a big brown engine coming toward him. He spoke as the engine drew near, "Hey, do you know when they will put me to work?" "When they are ready," huffed the brown engine. So little Engine Ninety-Nine continued to wait.

Just when he was sure he could wait no longer, a man in striped overalls came aboard. The man started the engine, and little Engine 99 was overwhelmed with joy. He began to move slowly. Then he picked up speed. Then he was breezing along the tracks. Wow! He loved the way the wind felt on his face.

After a while, the man pulled back on the controls and stopped the engine. He got out and switched the tracks. When the man returned, he started the engine again. This time, little Engine Ninety Nine felt himself being pulled forward, then backward, then forward, and then backward, until he heard CLINK! He was attached to some cars behind him. Little Engine Ninety Nine looked back, and sure enough, there were the elephants, the lions, the giraffe, and the bears he had dreamed of hauling. Now little Engine Ninety Nine is a working engine—exactly the kind of engine he'd dreamed that he would be.

Interesting Facts Related to Honk, Honk, Rattle, Rattle

Camels
- ○ Small animals can find shade and enough water and food easily, but for big animals it is much harder. The African dromedary camel helps people survive in the desert by carrying people and their belongings when they move from place to place.
- ○ Camels are able to live on very poor vegetation during the dry summer months. The fat stored in the hump will provide the camel with enough energy to reach better grazing areas.

○ Camels' eyes are protected by long eyelashes and have an extra, thin eyelid. In a desert sandstorm they can keep walking and still find their way. Camels' ears are small and very hairy, to keep flying sand from entering. Their nostrils can close completely or leave just a tiny opening for breathing.

Crocodiles

○ Crocodiles swim by moving their powerful tails from side to side. They can swim long distances and stay underwater for up to five hours.

○ Male crocodiles can weigh over a ton and measure over 16 feet in length. Female crocodiles rarely grow larger than 10 feet.

○ Crocodiles have very good vision; they can see almost 180 degrees but can't see anything below their nose.

○ Females build a big nest, which can a foot wide and two feet deep. They deposit 60-80 eggs in their nest and will defend the nest to the death from any and all animals.

○ When the mother crocodile hears the babies calling, she runs over to dig them out of the nest. She then carries her babies safely to the water in her mouth.

○ Crocodile eggs and baby crocodiles are eaten by water pythons, long-necked turtles, birds, and other crocodiles. From 500 eggs laid in the wild, only about two or three will become adult crocodiles.

Walking

○ The first person to walk on the moon was the American astronaut, Neil Armstrong. He set foot on the lunar surface on July, 21, 1969. His first words on the moon were "One small step for man, one giant leap for mankind." His footprints are still there because there's no wind or rain on the Moon.

○ If you walked at a steady speed of three mph non-stop day and night, it would take you a whole year to walk around the equator—a distance of 40,000 km (25,000 miles). The average person walks the equivalent of three and a half times around the earth in a lifetime.

Recipe

Gelatin Jigglers

Mix flavored gelatin with half the amount of water suggested on the box. Chill until it hardens. Cut into sailboat shapes or cut using transportation-related cookie cutters.

Bicycle Banana Wheels Rebus Recipe

(Using a rebus recipe makes it easier for English language learners to follow the directions.)

Bicycle Banana Wheels

Place 1 teaspoon of dry Jell-O in a ziplock bag.

Remove the bicycle banana wheels with toothpicks and eat.

Give the children plastic knives to slice bananas.

Encourage children to put 3 or 4 banana slices in bag and shake.

Marshmallow Train Rebus Recipe

(Using a rebus recipe makes it easier for English language learners to follow the directions.)

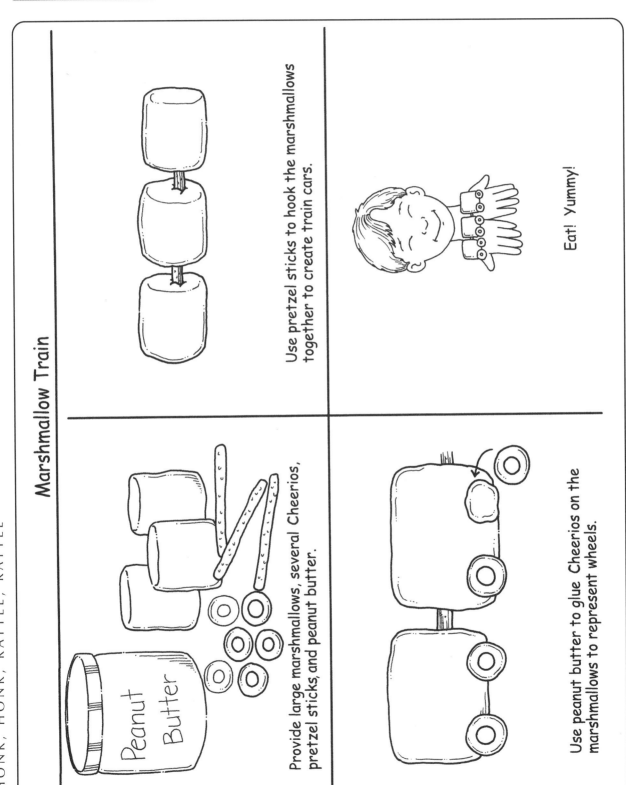

Marshmallow Train

Provide large marshmallows, several Cheerios, pretzel sticks, and peanut butter.

Use peanut butter to glue Cheerios on the marshmallows to represent wheels.

Use pretzel sticks to hook the marshmallows together to create train cars.

Eat! Yummy!

Twinkie Train Rebus Recipe

(Using a rebus recipe makes it easier for English language learners to follow the directions.)

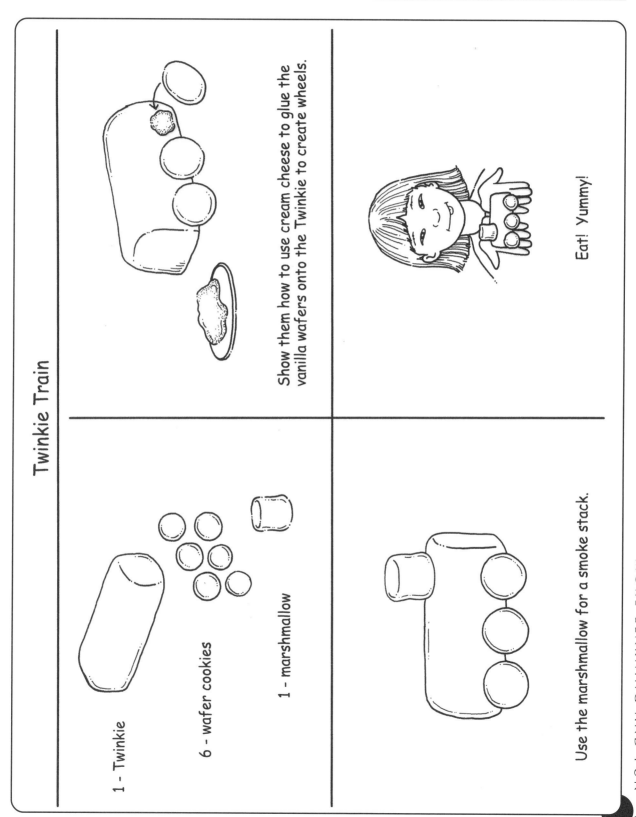

Twinkie Train

1 - Twinkie

6 - wafer cookies

1 - marshmallow

Use the marshmallow for a smoke stack.

Show them how to use cream cheese to glue the vanilla wafers onto the Twinkie to create wheels.

Eat! Yummy!

Venn Diagram

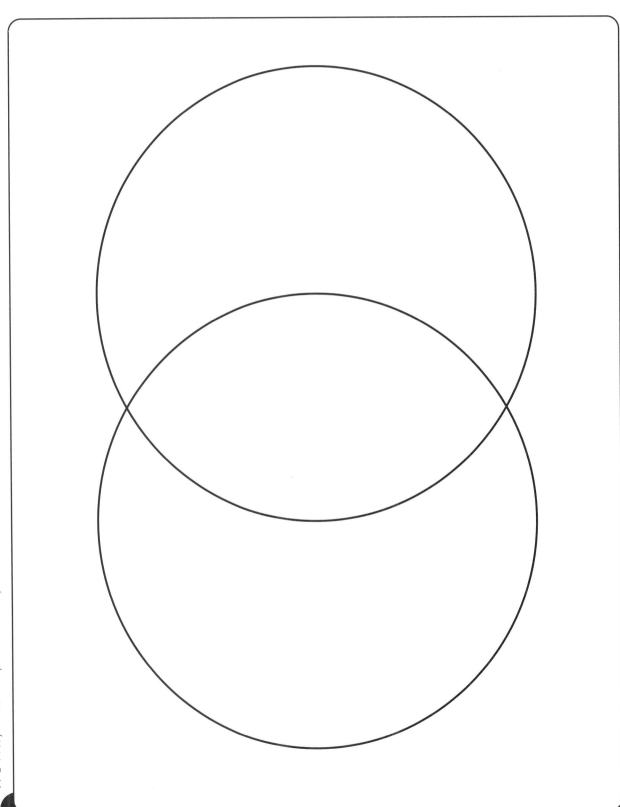

Camel Patterns

Camel Patterns

Camel Patterns

Finger Puppets

Flannel Board Patterns

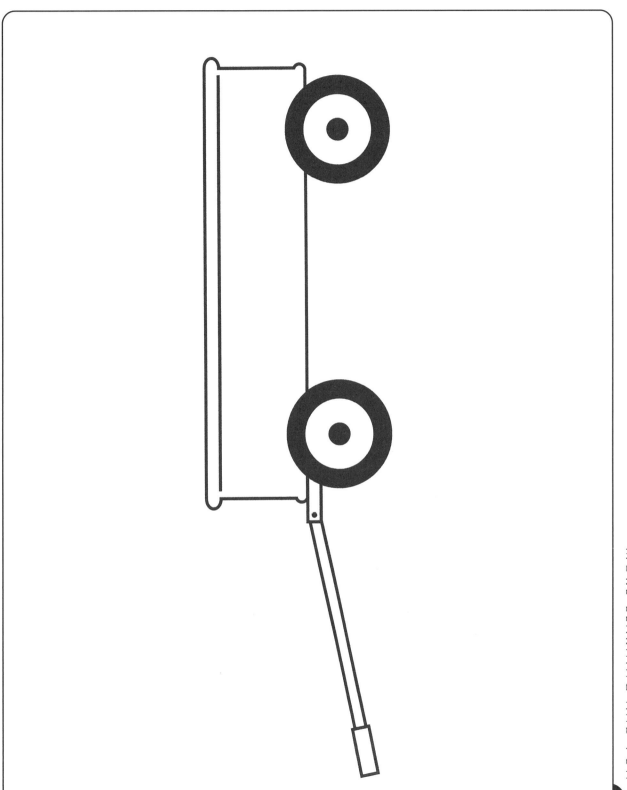

Flannel Board Patterns

plant

rock

toy car

dog

Pinwheel Pattern

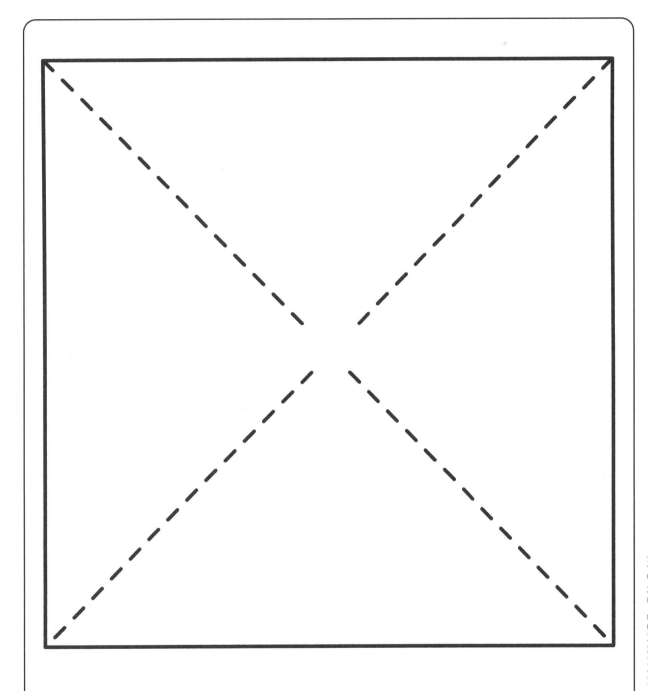

Sailboat Patterns

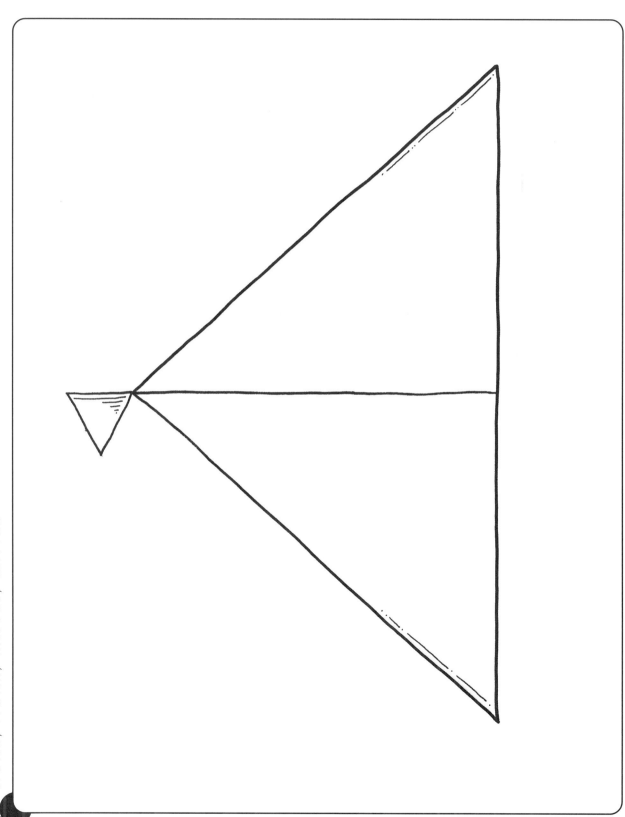

Sailboat Patterns

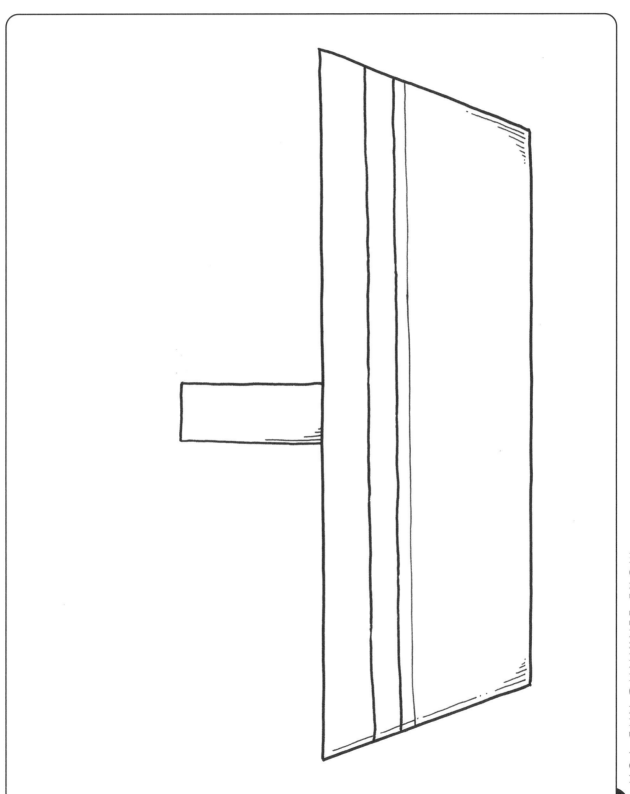

Train Patterns

Train Patterns

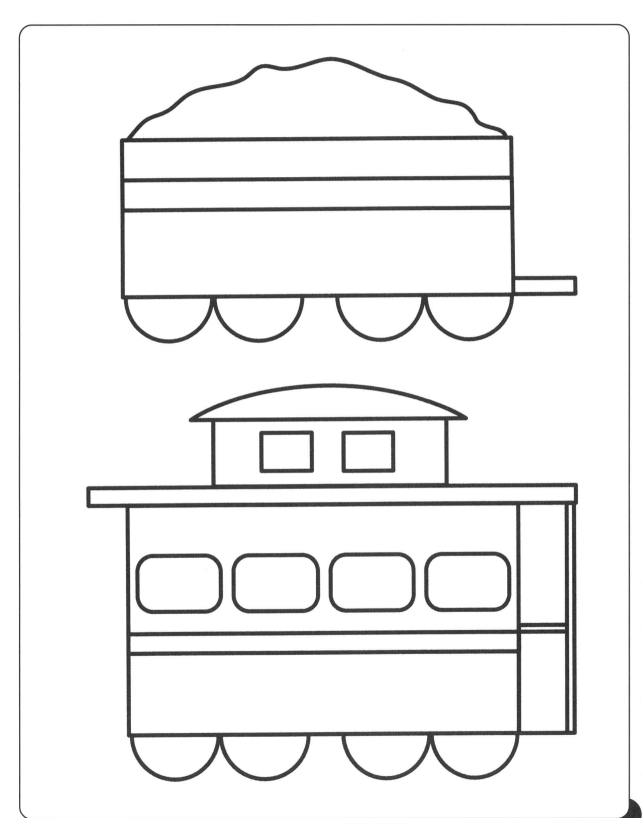

Color Word Rhyming Game

(red/bed, blue/shoe, black/sack, green/bean, brown/clown, gray/hay)

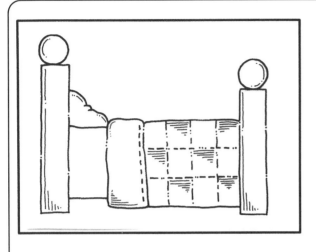 

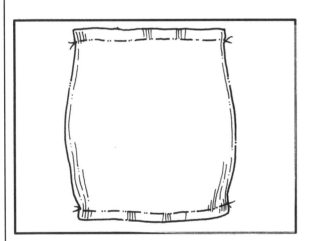 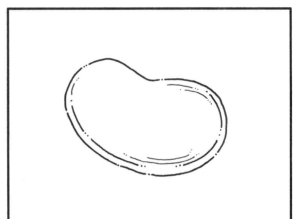

Color Word Rhyming Game

(red/bed, blue/shoe, black/sack, green/bean, brown/clown, gray/hay)

red	**black**
blue	**brown**
green	**gray**

Train Rhyming Word Cards

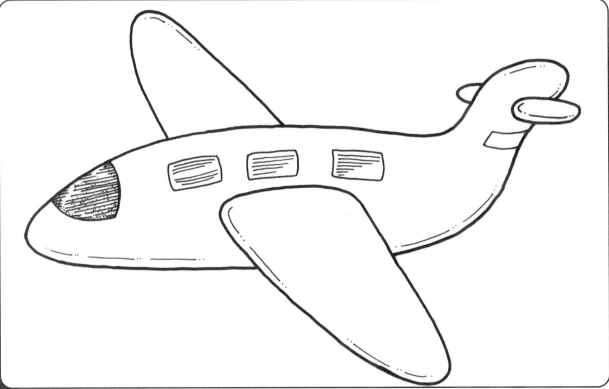

Train Rhyming Word Cards

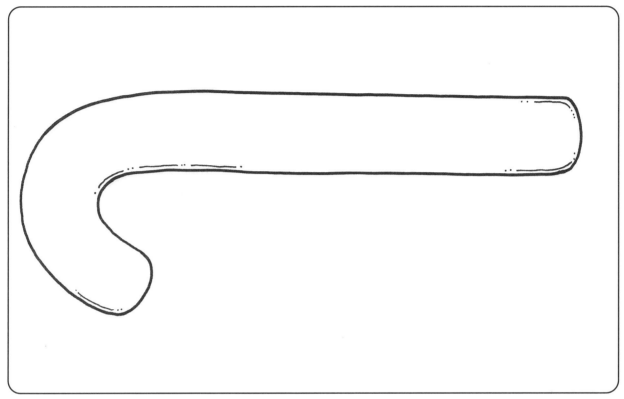

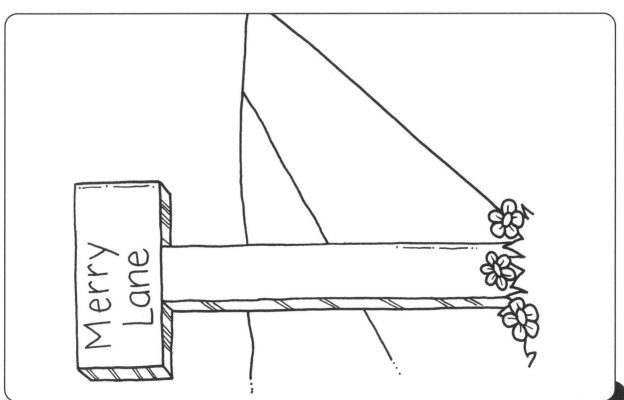

Train Rhyming Word Cards

Rebus Treasure Hunt

Clue #1

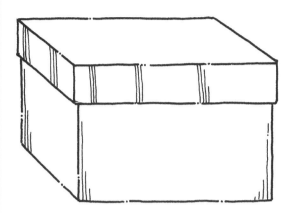

Come on, little pirates, be sly like a fox.
You'll find your first clue inside a box!

Clue #2

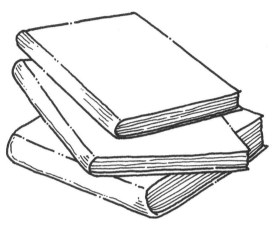

Look on the floor for books in a stack.
You'll find the next clue on a book back!

Clue #3

You're almost there—just one more clue.
Look closely beside the glue!

Clue #4

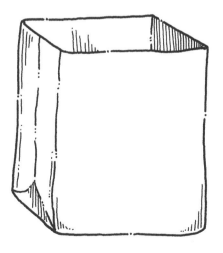

Turn three times and say, "Yippee."
The treasure you seek is right here with me!

American Sign Language Signs

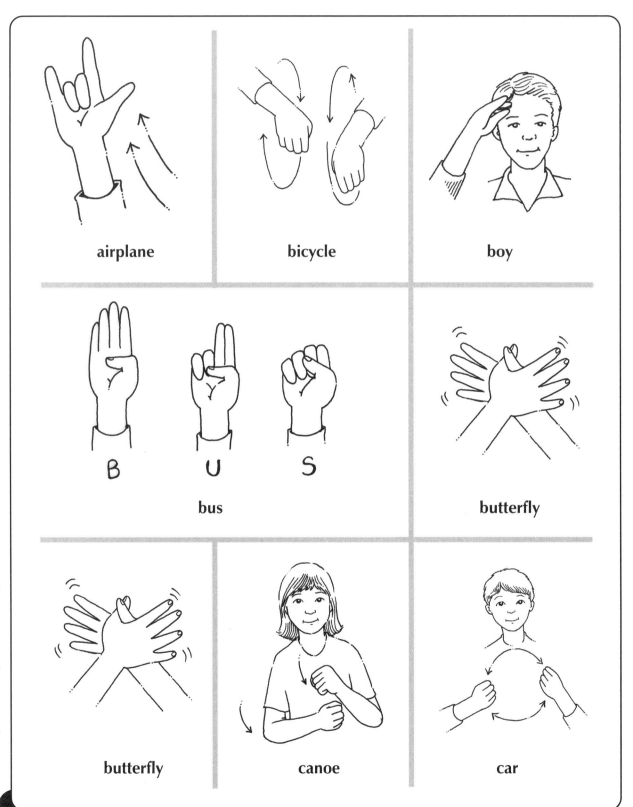

airplane

bicycle

boy

bus

butterfly

butterfly

canoe

car

American Sign Language Signs

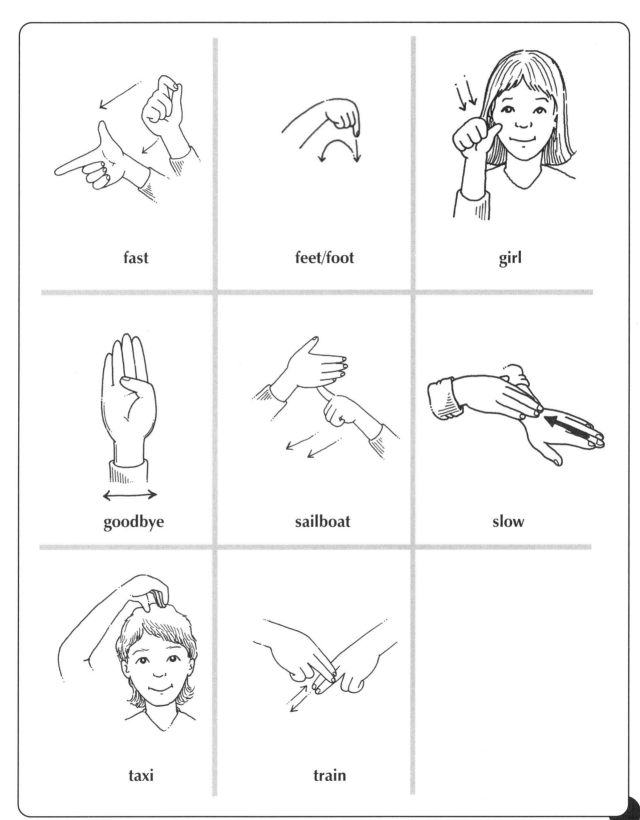

fast

feet/foot

girl

goodbye

sailboat

slow

taxi

train

References and Bibliography

Bulloch, K. 2003. *The mystery of modifying: Creative solutions*. Huntsville, TX: Education Service Center, Region VI.

Cavallaro, C. & M. Haney. 1999. *Preschool inclusion*. Baltimore, MD: Paul H. Brookes Publishing Company.

Gray, T. and S. Fleischman. Dec. 2004-Jan. 2005. "Research matters: Successful strategies for English language learners." *Educational Leadership*, 62, 84-85.

Hanniford, C. 1995. *Smart moves: Why learning is not all in your head*. Arlington, VA: Great Ocean Publications, p. 146.

Keller, M. 2004. "Warm weather boosts mood, broadens the mind." Ann Arbor, MI : Post Doctoral Study: The University of Michigan.

LeDoux, J. 1993. "Emotional memory systems in the brain." *Behavioral and Brain Research*, 58.

Theme Index

Children's Book Index

Index